Mindfulness
in the
Classroom

Mindfulness
in the
Classroom

Mindful Principles for Social
and Emotional Learning

Season Mussey, Ed.D.

Routledge
Taylor & Francis Group

NEW YORK AND LONDON

Library of Congress Cataloging-in-Publication Data

Names: Mussey, Season S., author.
Title: Mindfulness in the classroom : mindful principles for social and
  emotional learning / Season Mussey, Ed.D.
Description: Waco, TX. : Prufrock Press Inc., [2019] | Includes
  bibliographical references.
Identifiers: LCCN 2019006636 (print) | LCCN 2019007571 (ebook) | ISBN
  9781618218643 (eBook) | ISBN 9781618218636 (pbk.)
Subjects: LCSH: Affective education. | Mindfulness (Psychology) | Social
  learning. | Emotional intelligence--Study and teaching.
Classification: LCC LB1072 (ebook) | LCC LB1072 .M87 2019 (print) | DDC
  370.15/34--dc23
LC record available at https://lccn.loc.gov/2019006636

First published in 2019 by Prufrock Press Inc.

Published in 2021 by Routledge
605 Third Avenue, New York, NY 10017
2 Park Square, Milton Park, Abingdon, Oxon OX14 4RN

Routledge is an imprint of the Taylor & Francis Group, an informa business

Cover design by Micah Benson and layout design by Allegra Denbo

ISBN: 9781032143828 (hbk)
ISBN: 9781618218636 (pbk)

DOI: 10.4324/9781003236665

Dedication

To Max, my favorite.

Table of Contents

Acknowledgments

Teachers transform the world by transforming the lives of their students. My life has been transformed by the teachers who have selflessly served me. I have learned most from my ultimate teacher, Jesus, and I pray that I reflect His compassion and love in my interactions with others.

I admire and lift up all of my countless teachers and professors, and I wish I could thank each and every one of you by name and buy you a cup of coffee. But that would take a lifetime (and I shouldn't drink that much caffeine), so I'll just say to all of my teachers: I love you and thank you, especially Miss Linda, Mrs. Moore, Mrs. Armstrong, Mrs. Hill, Mr. Phillips, Mrs. Boyette, Mrs. Spencer, Dr. Wishard-Guerra, Dr. Ramsey, Dr. Levin, and Dr. Daly.

Similarly, I want to recognize all of my former, current, and future students. I've learned so much from you. I love you. Let me know what amazing things you are doing in your life.

Mom and Dad, my first teachers, you saw the teacher in me from the time I was 7 years old. From my first stapler, to my work ethic and perseverance, to the mighty machine that I am using to type these words today, you've always equipped me with the tools that I would need to succeed. I love you.

To my best brother Troy, my first student and friend: Thank you for supporting my adventures no matter what, especially in California. Thank you to my brother's loving wife, Reba, a dedicated principal and teacher leader. Thank you to Jonah, Jeremiah, Braiden, and Brielle for coming to Aunt Camp and trying my crazy crafts and science experiments. Thank you, Mimi, for your sweet words of encouragement. Thank you, Dean and Kris, for cheering me on. Thank you to all of my family members, near and far. Family is everything to me. I love you.

A special thank you to Jeremiah for consulting with me on kid-friendly definitions and ideas. His expertise and writing abilities were invaluable to me on this project. Jeremiah is 6.

To my dear friends, old and new: You bless my life. To Jaimee for sharing your heart and wisdom and for talking me through this process week after week: Thank you for sharing your story of empathy, a lesson for all of us to learn. Thank you, River, for your sweet heart. Thank you to Dr. Napoli for our transformative conversations: You believed in this project from the beginning. To Glenda, Beth, Jena, and my ladies: You hold me up.

Thank you, Paula, for telling me what I actually mean when I say what I *think* I mean, and for convincing me to stay in teaching. If it weren't for you, I might be studying bonobos in Africa right now, which would be cool, but not where I was meant to be . . . you knew.

Thank you, Bud, for being my mentor and friend. I treasure being your student and witness to your legacy.

Thank you for the lessons learned from all of my colleagues and leaders at TAMUCT and HT. Thank you for your kindness and professionalism, especially Deborah, Yvonne, Christina, Dorleen, and Brenda. Thank you, Dr. Seiter, my research partner and friend: You are a true professional educator and leader. Thank you, Dawson, my teaching partner and friend. Thank you to the entire science department and my friends at McCallum and Preuss, and thank you to the leadership at both of these fine institutions. What I learned at McCallum laid the foundation for much of what I do today. What I learned at

Acknowledgments

Preuss transformed the way that I think about the world. Thank you to my friends at AVID, Beth and Holly: You taught me about grace. Thank you to my yoga teachers and classmates for teaching me how to breathe: You still bring light to my life and the world. Thank you for my friends and coaches at Team in Training for teaching me discipline and commitment. Go Team!

Thank you to the friends and organizations that allow me the opportunity to do what I love and nurture my gift of teaching. Thank you especially to my friends at Woodlawn, Friendship International, and ISS.

Thank you to everyone who supports Kaya Teacher Project. This book will be foundational for the work that we do moving forward.

Thank you to the amazing team at Routledge for recognizing the potential of this project and for guiding me through this wonderful process. It has been a dream to work with you, and you have made it seem relatively easy. A special thank you to my editorial team, Katy McDowall and Stephanie McCauley. I have loved collaborating with you on this important work. Stephanie, your insight and thought-provoking (and kind) questioning style pushed my thinking and elevated the level of this work beyond what I imagined. Thank you to the sales team at Sourcebooks and everyone in your organiza-tion that has made this possible: You are a treasure and I hope that my efforts live up to your expectations.

Thank you to all of the teachers who will read this book. Thank you for using the ideas presented here to impact the lives of kids and make the world a better place for us all. I wish I could see all of the amazing things you will do, taking words on a page and putting them to action in your classroom. Your masterpiece awaits. You and the precious, beautiful students whom you serve are my "why."

Finally, my heart, my darling husband: Your calming presence is a blessing, and you remind me what matters most. I love you more. To my little Lulu, my muse: Thank you for letting Mommy "do her homework" and reminding me to "save my book." I hope you are proud of me. I am so very proud of you forever. This book is dedicated to you and your teachers. May they serve you well.

PART I

Mindfulness Matters

"Begin at the beginning," the King said, very gravely, "and go on till you come to the end: then stop."
　　　　—Lewis Carroll, *Alice's Adventures in Wonderland*

Pay Attention

"There was another school shooting today," my friend told me.

I already knew (Montgomery, Mele, & Fernandez, 2017), but I let her talk. My friend, a teacher, knew better than all of us what this meant. Fear. Questions. More students would be absent from her class tomorrow. Parent phone calls. E-mails. So many e-mails. Tears.

"What can I do?" she asked. We all ask.

In this book, you will find an answer, a response that is proactive and practical—a response that, if adopted by a critical mass, might facilitate change.

If attempted, we might be able to teach teachers, students, and ourselves how to be better humans, how to get along, how to ask for what we need, and how to respond to the needs of others. These lessons will teach us how to be better—delicately, appropriately, and in a way that ultimately elevates our humanity. If you are a classroom teacher, administrator, professor, school leader, teacher trainer, parent, student, or anyone who cares about schools and has a stake in the future of our world, this book is for you.

What I am suggesting in the following pages isn't rocket science, although there is science behind my methods. What I am suggesting is *mindfulness*, the conscious act of paying attention for a particular purpose. Mindfulness guru Jon Kabat-Zinn used the following operational definition of mindfulness: "the awareness that arises through paying attention, on purpose, in the present moment, non-judgmentally" (Foundation for a Mindful Society, 2017, para. 2).

Imagine a world where people are *paying attention*—to each other, to needs and hurts, to strengths, and to triumphs. Imagine a world where paying attention leads to appropriate responses: love, compassion, collaboration, celebration. Imagine a world where we pay attention so closely that we no longer ignore our hurting neighbor. Imagine a world where individuals possess tools that enable them to communicate and collaborate for the good of their communities. Imagine a classroom like this. What learning could take place if teachers and students were paying attention?

Mindfulness is paying attention. If you, like my teacher friend, have been paying attention, you have noticed that we must do something. I believe that implementing a mindfulness protocol into our schools could be a preventative action that will make people more selfless, more socially aware, more compassionate, and better human beings in general. It could be an avenue to support teachers as they teach, learners as they learn, and society as it evolves toward love, possibly preventing the kinds of devastating tragedies that have plagued our nation's schools and classrooms.

I believe that mindfulness is more than a buzzword in our system. I believe that it is a way to teach the social and emotional competence that students need to be successful in school and in life. I believe that the link between mindfulness and social and emotional learning

Mindfulness Matters

(SEL) has yet to be fully explored or utilized in our schools and is an untapped resource for student and teacher success.

Using mindfulness to promote both social and emotional competence isn't a revolutionary concept. Initial findings indicate that a mindfulness approach to SEL works and that teachers hold the key (Collaborative for Academic, Social, and Emotional Learning [CASEL], 2018a; Cullen, 2011; Kabat-Zinn, 2003; Schonert-Reichl, 2017; Sherretz, 2011; Tobin, 2018). There is merit to these pioneers' ideas, and this book provides teachers with a framework and the practical tools they need to practice mindfulness themselves.

Follow me on a journey toward mindful practice in the classroom. Let us explore eight principles of mindfulness as they are linked to social and emotional learning. Return to the heart of teaching the whole child as a human. Start with meeting students' human needs so that they might reach their academic potential as well. Reclaim your teaching heart. Return to yourself as a teacher, as a leader, and as a human desiring to make the world a better place.

Human Needs

As you may remember from Psychology 101, there is a hierarchy of human needs (McLeod, 2018). At the basic level, after our biological needs are met, social and emotional needs are foundational. Only after we address the matters of the heart can we achieve higher intellectual and cognitive pursuits. Until we address this social-emotional foundation, we will never get to the intellectual expansion that we strive for as educators.

Mindfulness, the art of paying attention with intention, is really a pathway to academic success. Before we can teach students algebra, we need to help them know that they are worth the time and effort that it will take to learn. They need to learn that relationships with their peers are worth time and effort. Let us help them understand that working together is as important as the math problem or the reenactment of Shakespeare. Let us instill in them a love for themselves and one another. Let us teach them the value of human life. Let us help them internalize practices that they need to thrive, regardless of the academic lesson they are learning. Let us give them life skills that they can carry with them into their future families and careers.

Our students are worth it, and so are you. I invite you to accompany me on this journey back to the heart of teaching and learning. Love will often be at the core of the principles I share with you. When we start to understand how to become more socially and emotionally aware and competent, we understand that we cannot move forward without love for one another.

Structure of the Book

In this book, we will explore eight principles of mindfulness practice and how they align with social and emotional learning. We will discover how the use of these practices increases student achievement in various contexts. For each principle, specific classroom strategies and activities are available for you to try.

This book is divided into three essential parts. Part I is the introduction, in which I give you a preview of the eight principles and an overview of how to use this book. Part II is devoted to discussing the eight principles. Each principle, expounded on in its own chapter, is grounded in theory and linked to practice. Part III is the conclusion, a call to action, and a discussion of implications for practice. My goal is to leave you reeling with ideas about how to move forward, share your newfound knowledge, and make the world a better place. I believe that if we do this work, it will matter. Mindfulness matters. As I write these pages, I dream of a better place for my children and yours. Will you join me?

How to Use
This Book

Efforts and courage are not enough without purpose and direction.

—John F. Kennedy

Disclaimer: I am not very good at following instructions or directions. Because I am a big-picture, visionary person, the details and step-by-step procedures never seem to interest me. However, whenever I attend a training, I count it worthwhile if I walk away with five or more practical ideas that I can implement the next day. So, as much as I'd rather talk about the theory and overarching concepts, once I buy into an idea, I know that I need the details in order to make anything happen.

The big picture and your purpose for teaching matter. Your purpose for teaching answers the questions, "Why do you teach? Why do you *want* to teach? What are some goals of your teaching practice?" We will call this your "why." Once you know your purpose and goals, you must determine how to proceed. In teaching, this includes developing pedagogical expertise by learning methods and strategies that

 DOI: 10.4324/9781003236665-2

will work to help you achieve your purpose. We can call these practices the "how" of teaching. I also refer to your collection of teaching methodologies and strategies as your teaching tool kit. The tools in your tool kit are the raw materials that you use to plan and deliver an effective lesson. Once you have a purpose and some methods at your disposal, you can act. Your first action might be to create a list of steps to follow, materials to gather, people to contact, resources to explore, or even papers to grade. The list dictates what you will do next, the "what." The "why," "how," and "what" of teaching are essential to being effective, but the "why" is your source of inspiration and hope. Teachers should start with "why" (Sinek, 2009) and revisit their "why" as their teaching careers progress. As you get further into the pages of this book, you will learn more about the concept of "why" as it relates to mindfulness in the classroom.

Before we get to the good stuff, I want to give you a road map and some tips for using this book effectively. If you are like me and would rather just jump in, I give you full permission to use this book in any way that makes sense for you. However, I have learned the hard way that not everyone out there is a big-picture kind of person. If you are one of those detail-oriented, "get it done" kind of folks, the rest of this chapter is for you.

From Principles to Practice

The remainder of Part I of this book provides some rationale and foundations that you will need to see the big picture of implementing mindfulness in your classroom. Part II of this book is divided into eight chapters. Each chapter is dedicated to a single mindfulness principle that will support social and emotional learning in the classroom. Within each chapter, you will read a description of the principle. You will also learn about the essential characteristics that make the principle work. Pay attention to the essentials (see Table 1).

Embedded within each principle is a discussion of how the principle may link to larger theories in educational research. Along the

How to Use This Book

TABLE 1

Mindfulness Principles and Their Essential Components

Principle	Essential Components
1. "I" Work	<ul><li>Be true; be you.</li><li>Know who you are.</li><li>Motivate others and yourself.</li></ul>
2. Creativity	<ul><li>Creativity must be practiced and cultivated.</li><li>Creativity takes time.</li><li>Creativity is inclusive.</li><li>Creativity takes courage.</li></ul>
3. Cultivating Connections	<ul><li>Be humble.</li><li>Be gentle.</li><li>Be patient.</li><li>Practice empathy.</li><li>Practice compassion.</li><li>Be peaceful.</li><li>Promote unity.</li></ul>
4. Writing	<ul><li>All teachers are writing teachers.</li><li>Writing is a process.</li><li>Writing is personal.</li></ul>
5. Breathing and Movement	<ul><li>Conscious breathing is slow.</li><li>Conscious breathing is deep.</li><li>Conscious breathing is rhythmic.</li><li>Move first.</li><li>Move for flexibility, stability, and strength.</li></ul>
6. Gratitude	<ul><li>Gratitude is simple.</li><li>Gratitude builds health.</li><li>Gratitude brings joy.</li><li>Gratitude improves the strength of relationships.</li></ul>
7. Holding Space	<ul><li>The space belongs to students (and you, but mostly them).</li><li>Holding space occurs in a positive classroom environment.</li><li>Holding space is an art.</li></ul>
8. Commit-to-One	<ul><li>Commitment shows what you believe.</li><li>Commitment shows what you value.</li><li>Commitment opens doors.</li><li>Commitment leads to success.</li></ul>

way, you will periodically find boxes entitled "Try This." These boxes contain practical activities that you can use to apply the principles in your real life. Some of the activities are for teachers or other adults who teach or train people. Some of the activities are for use with your students. Some activities are individual reflections. There are a variety of ideas to try, and I encourage you to jump in. Try one thing at a time and reflect on the outcome.

At the end of each chapter, you will find a list of discussion questions and a journal prompt. These questions and writing prompts are designed to help you internalize what you have read in a real way. Some of the discussion questions are metacognitive reflections, and some are practical ideas to try.

In the Appendix, you will find outlines for lesson plans that could be used in the classroom. Each lesson plan relates to one of the eight principles. All of the activities and ideas are adaptable, and you should use your experience and expertise to ensure that you are applying ideas in age-appropriate, ethical ways. All of the lesson plans are suitable for multiple grade levels and age levels when scaffolding is provided. Scaffolding includes making the needed modifications and adaptations to meet all learning needs, literacy levels, learning styles, etc. Use these lesson plan outlines and apply best practices, especially practices that you know work in your learning context. If you don't think that a lesson plan will work for your class or grade level, change it or try a different one.

The remainder of this chapter is divided into three sections, each written for a specific audience. The first section is for the classroom teacher and other adults who work directly with children. The second section is for individuals who train teachers, primarily adults who work with other adults (e.g., teacher educators, university professors, professional developers, school administrators, instructional facilitators). The last section is for all readers.

How to Use This Book: For Teachers

Teachers, spend most of your time with Part II of the book. Read about the mindfulness principles and pay close attention to the essentials and the "Try This" sections. Try the activities and let me know how they go! Incorporate these activities into your lesson planning or daily schedule as you see fit. There are more than 50 activities at your disposal. Find the lesson plans in the Appendix. Read and adapt the plans to your teaching context.

Notice that in each chapter, there is a discussion of how the mindfulness principle relates to social and emotional learning. There are five categories of SEL competencies: self-awareness, self-regulation, social awareness, relationship-building skills, and decision-making skills (CASEL, 2018c). Any direct connections to one or more of the competencies will be made explicit and included in the chapter.

At the end of each chapter is a list of discussion questions as well as a journal prompt. Use these when conducting a systematic review of this book or a book study. Use these individually or with colleagues in your professional learning community to enhance your understanding of the text.

As a teacher, it is important to notice when and how social-emotional learning might help you, when it might help your students, and when it impacts the classroom environment. All three areas of application were considered for each principle. All three considerations are essential for wide implementation of SEL in a classroom or on a campus (Schonert-Reichl, 2017). For each principle, I systematically explored several questions, listed in Figure 1. I encourage you to use this list of questions to explore and apply each mindfulness principle to your practice.

SEL for Teachers

1. How does the mindfulness principle help teachers develop their own social and emotional competence?
2. How can teachers apply the knowledge and skills they gain from practicing this mindfulness principle to their work with students?
3. How can teachers implicitly model the essentials of the principle?
4. How can teachers explicitly teach the essentials of the principle?

SEL for Students

1. How can students use the mindfulness principle to develop social and emotional competence?
2. How can students internalize and use the essentials of the mindfulness principle in their interactions with adults and their student peers?
3. How does application and utilization of the mindfulness principle influence students' academic performance?

A Classroom Environment for SEL

1. What special considerations must be made to the classroom environment to promote using the mindfulness principle for social and emotional learning?
2. How does the mindfulness principle positively affect the classroom environment?

FIGURE 1. Questions to explore for each mindfulness principle.

How to Use This Book: For Teacher Educators

There is only one thing that I love more than teaching students: teaching teachers! If you are blessed to call yourself a teacher trainer or professional developer, there are many ways that you can use this book.

This book would be an excellent supplemental text for a methods class in any content area. The eight principles can be embedded into content instruction and classroom procedures. However, novice teachers need you to show them how to integrate all of the ideas that they are learning. The most important way to "show" them is to model these ideas yourself.

Another use of this book would be to support the development of action research projects for teachers in classrooms. Consider helping teachers design a preassessment and a postassessment to measure changes after implementation of a specific principle or idea. Of course, for many of the principles, the evidence collected will be anecdotal or observational. Use this book to develop qualitative research questions and discover the effectiveness of these concepts for yourself.

Finally, you can apply the ideas in this book to create a culture of mindfulness within your organization. This book is meant to inspire preservice and inservice teachers to do their best work. To do that, I would suggest using the book in a campus- or districtwide professional development training. This book can also inspire teacher trainers. Consider using this book in departmental meetings or over a series of brown-bag lunches. Meet once a week and explore one of the eight principles each week. Encourage one another to apply each principle to various contexts and report back. Share successes and learning outcomes. Support one another as you work on supporting a paradigm shift in our field. Consider the potential for major ripple effects as you teach those who teach others.

How to Use This Book: For Everyone

Each chapter in Part II of this book is about one of the principles that make up the mindfulness teaching framework. Mindfulness principles are for everyone. Mindfulness helps people develop self-awareness, self-regulation, social awareness, relationship skills, and decision-making skills. We all need more of these skills and abilities in our lives. We all need to attend to these ideas for ourselves and for the people with whom we interact daily.

In Summary

This book is for everyone. We are nothing if not inclusive, and I certainly hope that you will find what you are looking for in the pages that follow.

Discussion Questions

1. Consider the relationship of the "why," "how," and "what" of classroom teaching. We often get caught up in our long to-do lists before we understand why or how to proceed. What is one way to address this issue?

2. In this chapter, I discussed the importance of applying mindfulness and SEL in three ways: for teachers, for students, and for the classroom environment. What is one way that SEL improves teacher performance? What is one way that SEL improves student behavior? What is one way that SEL can improve the classroom environment or the learning space?

Journal Prompt

When you approach a project, are you more of a big-picture or detail-oriented person? Describe the benefits of your approach as it applies to your current role at work. Discuss the drawbacks of your approach. Think of someone in your life who balances your perspective (e.g., if you are a big-picture person, think of a detail-oriented person). How could you work with that person to accomplish your goals? Consider reaching out to that person as you explore the chapters that follow. How could you work together to apply this mindfulness framework to your work and lives?

Mindfulness for Teaching and Learning

The Foundations

If you have built castles in the air, your work need not be lost; that is where they should be. Now put the foundations under them.

—Henry David Thoreau

Technology Today: The Need for Speed

My 2-year-old son can find his monster truck songs on any electronic device in a matter of seconds. He amazes me. I wonder if he can already read and write; how else could he maneuver these thousand-dollar devices with such skill and accuracy? Unlike me, he uses technology effortlessly. Unlike me, who (gasp) didn't even have a cell phone *or* Google in college, he was born with a device in his hand. He is a native technology user, like our students. If I would allow it, he would mindlessly sit, staring and pushing buttons for days.

Technology is cool; technology is fast. As a bibliophile, I love this. I can access thousands of books at my fingertips anytime, day or

 DOI: 10.4324/9781003236665-3

night. In fact, sometimes I feel guilty when I stop to do something else. Shouldn't I be learning? Shouldn't I be consuming? Shouldn't I be staring at my phone for hours at a time? The value of mindless consumption is a dangerous lie that we have been learning and teaching our youth. It is a lie that we need to stop telling.

The fact that technology has accelerated at an astounding rate is no surprise to the tech industries. Gordon Moore predicted the pace of the digital revolution when he studied the rate of increase of transistor use in a dense integrated circuit (Intel, n.d.). As predicted, in what has come to be known as Moore's Law, the growth rate has been exponential. From 1971 to 2016, technology moved at an exponential pace. As technology continues to grow—at a predictable rate with unpredictable outcomes—humanity has tried to keep up.

Quiet moments of reflection are not part of the fabric of our current existence, nor are they intuitive. Not too long ago, the world moved at a slower pace. There were days when it took minutes or hours rather than nanoseconds to download information. We were forced to wait. It was frustrating, but there were benefits, too. The mandatory pauses built into our daily tasks required us to take deep breaths and be patient. Technology's sluggishness literally helped us slow down.

As wonderfully convenient and fast as today's technology is, we no longer have the luxury of this automatic pause. If the world had its way, we would always go, never pausing to ask why or how or *if* we should be moving at all. Let's pause here for a moment of reflection. Consider the last time that you did absolutely nothing. (Sleep doesn't count.)

TRY THIS: The Do-Nothing Activity

Find a place to sit. Do nothing. Do nothing for 5 whole minutes. Do not look at your phone or watch TV. Do not talk. Try not to think. Do nothing. Enjoy.

Mindfulness for Teaching and Learning

The world needs mindfulness. As the pace of our technology-driven world quickens, and we can access anything at our fingertips in a matter of seconds, we must prioritize being still. We must learn to pause in the midst of the dizzying chaos of our lives and ask, "What is going on here? How are things going? How are you? How am I?"

I imagine, for most of us, these moments of pause and nothingness are rare and strange.

Mindfulness for Teachers

Mindfulness could be considered an intentional moment of doing nothing. But a moment of nothing, if followed by something wonderful, would be worth it, wouldn't it? I can attest that when you practice stillness for long enough the guilt goes away, acceptance comes, and the wonderful productivity that follows is astounding.

When I am mindful, I am aware of my physical, social, and emotional space. I can pause in this awareness and find clarity. Judgment, criticism, and confusion fall away. Observation remains, and I can see clearly. Clarity allows for rational decision making.

There are few who need this practice more than professional educators. Did you know that teachers make, on average, 1,500 decisions every single day (TeachThought Staff, 2016)? That means that classroom teachers make approximately four decisions per minute. Although not all decisions are life and death, some are. Teachers need clarity, time, and space to decipher which decisions are significant and which ones necessitate a mere nod of the head or raise of the eyebrow. Teachers, more than anyone, need permission to pause and be mindful in the midst of the noise.

Teachers Matter

Tupac Shakur (as cited in Educate Inspire Change TV, 2014) once said, "I'm not sayin' I'm gonna change the world, but I guarantee that I will spark the brain that will." When I taught seventh-grade science, I used to think, "What if the cure to cancer lies in the mind of one of my Axe-wearing, attitude-bearing, SpongeBob-loving students?" With that in mind, I could approach each day with a sense of importance and urgency. Regardless of the inevitable middle school drama and silliness that would cross my path, I knew that what we were doing mattered in the world. I needed to be the best teacher that I could be because I was planting the seeds that would germinate, grow, and produce fruit one day. I had to make a difference in my students' lives so that they could make a difference in the world.

TRY THIS: Thank-You Notes—Teacher Edition

Think about a teacher who made a difference in your life. Notice that I didn't say the "best teacher" or the "most effective." Instead choose a teacher who mattered to you. Write a thank-you note to that person now. This is mine:

Dear Mrs. Spencer,

On the day that we dissected a fetal pig, you wore a pink dress, pink tights, and a matching pink headband with pig ears. Your costume and zeal for learning inspired me then and even now. I'm sure there were days when you faked it, but we never knew. You were the first person who said I could be organized as I proudly cut and pasted color-coded notes into my interactive spiral. You talked to me about college. You believed that I could go. You trusted me and my 16-year-old peers with scalpels and gel electrophoresis. You are the reason my 1985 Toyota truck was invaded by fruit flies. You forced us to be mindful about our learning and our futures. You are the reason that I still teach today. I can never thank you enough. I love you.

Your student always,
Season

Mindfulness for Teaching and Learning

Teachers matter. If you take anything from reading this text, take that. I thank the teachers who devote themselves to their students and their practice, and I honor them with this work. If I could, I would shower every teacher out there with unending gratitude.

But gratitude is not enough. Teaching is hard. There are so many demands on the classroom teacher that we often lose the good teachers before they get good. In a meta-analysis of 34 research studies on teacher attrition, Borman and Dowling (2008) found that there are many reasons for this trend. Teachers cite adverse work conditions, such as lack of resources, organizational issues, and inability to contribute to decision making. Moreover, the teachers who are leaving are often the better qualified, better trained, and more experienced individuals who are truly needed in our schools. If we were losing ineffective teachers, a kind of "healthy attrition," then this trend might not cause alarm. Unfortunately, we are often losing the best of the best. The good news from this landmark study is that we can influence teachers to persist. In this book, we consider how to use mindfulness and SEL to support teachers as they pursue longevity in the field.

What tools do teachers need to persist past those first survival years? What tools do they need to become masters of their craft? There are many. We know that effective teachers must have subject matter expertise, theoretically grounded teaching methodologies and pedagogical expertise, lesson planning skills, classroom management strategies, and an assessment plan (Marzano, 2007). Teachers need to be organized. Teachers must learn and comply with laws, policies, rules, and cultural norms of behavior. Teachers must be masterful communicators with myriad diverse stakeholder groups. We know that they must mind their behavior on social media, remaining ethical at all times. They are held to a high moral standard in society (Association of American Educators, n.d.). Teachers must even be mindful about what they put in their grocery cart. People are always watching.

University-based and alternative teacher preparation programs are doing their best to equip teachers with internships, mentoring, and practicums that will help prepare them for the realities that they will face. But it is a challenge. Teaching is hard, and there will never be enough preservice preparation for the day when the classroom teacher finds herself alone in a room with 42 pairs of adolescent eyes staring back at her. Teachers need time to collaborate and support one another (Mosle, 2014). The preparation programs could never even imagine all of the scenarios that the classroom teacher will encounter. Teaching is hard, and it is a lifelong practice of learning and growth.

Teaching Practice

Teaching requires practice. There is a reason that we are called *practitioners*. Like doctors, we take our advanced training and practicum experience and apply it on a case-by-case basis. We administer diagnostic preassessments and prescribe individualized treatments in the form of learning plans. We use a cycle of instructional improvement, applying data from formative assessments to our lesson design. It takes at least 3–5 years to even gain a foothold in this work, and it takes even longer to become a master teacher and find your voice (Johnson, 2016). Teachers need support during this time of development. Like doctors, teachers cannot afford to make life-threatening mistakes. They must have relevant resources and the right tools to guide them.

Watzke's (2007) research made the case for reflective practice and ongoing professional development as a way to help teachers learn how to improve their practice. Johnson (2016) described the three phases in attitude development that teachers move through: shock, cynicism, and, finally, self-actualization. There is need for a shift away from negativity toward an attitude of growth. Carol Dweck (2006) started a mindset movement, offering insight into the importance of a growth mindset for transformation of self and students.

In order to put such research into practice, teachers need to practice principles of mindfulness prior to stepping foot in the classroom. It is not possible to be ready for every teaching scenario; however, teachers must be ready to learn. They must be ready to pay attention to what they are doing, how they are doing, and how they can improve. They must enter their work with a growth mindset, believing that they can get better. To do this, teachers need preparation in mindful practices.

When they are ill-prepared, teachers leave the profession (Borman & Dowling, 2008; Schaefer, Downey, & Clandinin, 2014). The cost of losing so many highly qualified, certified teachers is astronomical. From 1999–2000, the estimated cost of replacing teachers who left the profession, not including the retirees, was nearly $2.2 billion (Borman & Dowling, 2008). This is not only a loss of financial capital, but also a waste of intellectual capital. Consider the time and effort that must be put into training a new teacher in a new school context. Time is a limited and precious resource in our school system, and we cannot afford to waste it. We must find a way to reverse this trend. Teachers need support, and teachers need mindfulness.

Mindfulness for Students

The only population that needs mindfulness more than the teachers are the students they serve. My 2-year-old is already a technological wizard. The speed of the technology that he will use in his lifetime is beyond my comprehension. Given this reality, how will the learners of his generation ever learn to slow down if we don't teach them? Mindfulness is paying attention and slowing down long enough to pay attention well.

I love kids. I went into this business for the kids. If you are reading this, then I am sure that you do, too. Nelson Mandela (1995) said, "There can be no keener revelation of a society's soul than the way in which it treats its children." Kids should be at the center of everything we do in schools, and they should be at the heart of every single one of our 1,500 daily decisions.

We must think about kids' futures. We must teach the skills and behaviors that they will need to solve the problems that lie ahead. We must prepare them for more than the standardized test at the end of the year. I've heard it said that we are preparing kids for technologies that don't yet exist. In this uncertainty, how must we proceed? Mindfully.

What are the skills that people will need to exercise their humanity in a world of machines? How can we help them practice being human in a world that values a text message more than face-to-face conversation? How can we teach them that human life is precious, despite what they see on the news? Mindfully.

It is important to be kind, honest, compassionate, and patient. How can we teach students to love one another as they love themselves? How can we teach them to love themselves regardless of how many "likes" they get on Instagram or Facebook? Mindfully.

Students need mindfulness. They need to practice paying attention with intention, and they need to learn these skills in the context of what will support their social and emotional growth. We can no longer ask or expect others to teach them. We are the adults. We must do the work.

Starting Over: Reimagining Your Teaching Practice

When I started to work on incorporating mindfulness into my teaching practice, I was teaching science to seventh graders in Southern California. Back then, I didn't know that I was teaching mindfulness. The term wasn't on my radar just yet.

To be honest, my first mindful moment grew from a state of quiet desperation. I was struggling daily, and I knew that I needed to do something in order to survive. At this point in my career, I had been teaching for 6 years. Although I loved kids and I loved science, my passion for teaching was slowly being extinguished by the pressure of the bureaucracy, the paperwork, and the reality of dealing with the insane range of hormones produced by the 12-year-olds in my room. I didn't understand why I hadn't "gotten good" at this teaching thing yet.

Mindfulness for Teaching and Learning

One day, I heard my students laughing, and I literally ran out of the classroom gasping for breath. I was having a physical reaction to the emotional strain of dealing with constant chaos and adolescent angst. I nearly threw up. I stood against a brick wall, allowing the building to hold me up. I counted to 10. I stayed there for a few minutes in disbelief.

What on earth had happened to me? The only thing that I knew was that I was sick and tired. I had literally retched at the noise of laughter and stormed out of the room for air. When did my body start rejecting the joyful noise of a child? Something was wrong. On the way home from school that day, I cried. I needed answers.

When I got home that night, I stopped crying. I reflected on what I had been doing and what I needed to change. I made a vow to myself that I would be better. I made a plan to start over. I believe that this is something that teachers must do often, reinventing themselves and their methods, rewriting their plans, and starting again. Tomorrow is always a new day.

So, I started over. The next day I began my class with a song about science. I set aside a time for jokes—science ones, of course. Laughter was written into my plan. On this new day, the students' laughter made me laugh, too. I apologized for not giving them my best. I explained how I had become "sick and tired." I made a vow to my students that I would be better.

I created a self-assessment for my students, asking them what was making them "sick and tired." What was making them go home and cry? Ultimately, the assessment rubric and the conversation that followed were about self-awareness and self-improvement. They were also about how to make our community and learning environment better, and about the power of paying attention. I told my students that we were starting over, and we did. It wasn't pretty or systematic, but it was a start. Mindfulness matters. This initial foray into the world of mindfulness and SEL was all I needed to catalyze the work that was to come.

TRY THIS: Joke of the Day

Jokes are wonderful avenues for self-expression. Consider allowing a time for jokes in your classroom. Create a joke rubric. Evaluate students on the quality of the jokes and their presentation. Give them points for originality and style. And don't forget to laugh.

Here are my two favorite science jokes of all time:

* A mushroom walks into a bar (or restaurant, if you are telling this to kids). The staff won't serve him. He says, "Why not? I'm a fungi (fun guy)?"
* Two atoms go shopping. One atom said to the other, "I think I left one of my electrons in the last store." Her friend says, "Are you sure?" She answers, "Yes, I'm positive."

In Summary

As you reflect on your teaching practice, consider the ways in which mindful principles can be incorporated into your work. Consider what is making you and your students sick and tired. What is making you cry? What do you need to start over?

Discussion Questions

1. Define mindfulness as you currently understand it.
2. In what two areas of your teaching practice could you use more mindfulness?
3. In what ways have you observed students acting without thinking? How could you help them pay attention in these areas? What would be the benefit to them?
4. Think of a teacher who helped you develop socially, emotionally, and academically. How was that person's approach different or better than that of other teachers you had?

Mindfulness for Teaching and Learning

Journal Prompt

Consider the concept of starting over in education. What is something that you wish you could start over? What needs to change? What do you have control over changing? Write a plan for change and pick a day on the calendar when you will "start over" in this area.

A Mindfulness Framework

I advocate using mindfulness in the classroom as a method to increase overall teacher effectiveness, student achievement, and the joy of teaching and learning. Adding a mindfulness framework around your existing subject matter and pedagogical expertise will serve to increase academic, social, and emotional learning. Before moving further into the text, consider preassessing your feelings, attitudes, and prior knowledge about mindfulness. This will act as a foundation for the rest of the chapter and book.

TRY THIS: Principle Preassessment

Pause for a moment and reflect on the following questions:
1. What do I already know or think I know about mindfulness and teaching?
2. What training have I received about teaching the whole child? How am I using what I know?
3. What fears or biases come up when I hear the word *mindfulness*?
4. What do I need to know to make my teaching better?

 DOI: 10.4324/9781003236665-4

Prior Knowledge, Misconceptions, and Hooey

As you reflect on your answers to the Try This: Principle Pre-assessment, one of two things may have come up for you. You may have realized that you already have many tools for using mindfulness at your disposal. If you do, bravo! Please keep doing the awesome work that you are doing, and please keep reading, as there is always more to learn.

If you've never heard of this mindfulness stuff, or you are being forced to read this book against your will as a part of a class or book study, you may have a different reaction. In my experience, skeptics respond with something like this: "Hooey. Mindfulness is a bunch of hooey." There is always some pushback when I start talking about mindfulness. Sometimes, my listeners' eyes glaze over. They start to think about their to-do lists. They grumble about how they don't have time for chanting and meditation when there are so many papers to grade.

You may be surprised to learn that mindfulness involves no chanting and no hooey. I do advocate using meditation as a tool for mindfulness. But did you know that if you've ever thought deeply about your teaching or engaged in any reflective practice activities, you've already been meditating? *Meditation*, or deep reflection and contemplative thought on a particular matter, helps us focus and gain perspective. Meditation helps us pay attention. When coupled with breathing techniques, there are a host of other benefits, which you will read about later. Ultimately, meditation is an effective tool, and, like the other principles and activities that I offer in this text, I'd love for you to try it if you think it will make you a better teacher. In fact, all that you will find in these pages is sound theory and sincere practices that were included to support you as you nurture students and facilitate academic learning in your classroom. If you try some of the activities, you might find that principles of mindfulness, when practiced, make

A Mindfulness Framework

your life and the lives of those around you better. Mindfulness practices might even make grading those papers easier to bear.

Ultimately, I hope this book will begin a conversation in your classroom and on your campuses. Conversations start movements, and as we move toward using mindfulness to teach self-awareness, social awareness, regulation, and decision making, we are reframing our work in education. We are moving toward a more compassionate society full of people who care about themselves and others. That is a movement that I want to join. You are already on the front lines, teaching and leading the next generation to greatness. The world needs you to continue making strides in your teaching practice and leading others to do the same. Your students need you to keep building your teacher tool kit. As you develop more subject matter knowledge and pedagogy, consider what else must go into your teaching practice as well as expected results. Regardless of what you already know and do, there is always more to learn. Let's learn more and do this work together.

TRY THIS: Social Contract

The following agreement includes four simple yet important statements that I present to my workshop participants. I ask you, as a reader of this book participating in the exercise of learning new strategies for classroom success, to agree to these, too. Please complete the following contract. Consider implementing this or a similar social contract in your classroom.

I, _____ (sign your name), agree to the following:
   1.   No criticism. (Try it before you judge it.)
   2.   No fear. (Be brave. Be bold.)
   3.   Be better together. (Collaborate and listen.)
   4.   Have some fun! (Look for the joy.)

Teachers as Leaders and Champions

The work of becoming a teacher leader begins now. Think back to the teacher whom you thanked earlier in this book. What made that person so special? Was it the artful way that she introduced calculus? Do you remember the realistic cellular respiration diagram that he drew? Perhaps, but it's doubtful. More likely you remember some of the following traits that made that teacher successful:

» **Teachers bring love into their work and into the world.** I imagine that many of you would say that the teacher you thanked loved you. Students remember the teachers that loved them.

» **Teachers are significant.** We often remember the difference-makers. You might say that a teacher helped you in an important, life-changing way. Some of you don't remember a thing that person taught, but you may remember the exact words of wisdom he or she spoke. You remember how that person made you feel. The teachers that we remember, either for their academic prowess or their encouragement, are significant to us.

» **Teachers are authors.** One of my favorite teachers always said, "Find the place where you can insert the lever of change" (H. Mehan, personal communication, 2008). Before I heard this advice, I had decided that making change was nearly impossible. I had almost given up. This teacher reminded me that I mattered. I had a sphere of influence, and I could make change in my sphere once I found the place to insert the lever. He was the author of an idea for me.

» **Teachers have power.** When I was in graduate school, I went to see one of my favorite teachers who was also my academic counselor. I wanted to make a difference in the world, but I didn't think that I was on the right path. I was overwhelmed by the challenges in the field of education, and the more I learned, the more impossible teaching seemed. I was strongly considering jumping off of the education boat. My counselor

A Mindfulness Framework

gently reminded me how many students I served annually. We did some math. Over a career, I would influence so many. She empowered me to stay in the boat and use my power for good.

Consider the qualities listed above: *love, significance, authorship, and power*. Bolman and Deal (2001) spoke about these four qualities as qualities of leadership. Although attention to these leadership qualities is rare, it is also necessary. When used together, these qualities result in profound and life-changing experiences. When I think about love, significance, authorship, and power, I see the heart of a teacher. Teachers must be mindful in what they do and how they are using these and other leadership qualities to promote profound change in the lives of the people they serve. Teachers need to think of themselves as leaders—leaders who give love, significance, authorship, and power to others.

A special teacher is someone who sees the potential in others. These kinds of teachers recognize the gifts rather than the flaws in their students. They seek to serve and do not condemn their students for what they do not know. Rather, they teach them. Teachers who pay attention to students' strengths create opportunities for students to be authentic. In their classes, students learn to have integrity and to be themselves. These special teachers refuse to compromise their values for what the "system" demands.

Teachers must be mindful about how to encourage integrity of identity for themselves and their students. When they do so, teachers become champions for themselves and their students. As Rita Pierson (2013) expressed, "every child deserves a champion." Champions inspire, and that inspiration becomes a motivator for others. Inspiration sustains motivation. Inspiring students tends to have a much more positive affect than the alternative and traditional motivation method of manipulation (Sinek, 2009). When teachers are mindful, manipulation and token economies become less valuable, and the real work of learning can begin.

The Real Work: Using Mindfulness to Inspire Learning

We are in the business of teaching and learning. To teach is to learn; to learn is to teach. Beyond providing instruction in academic areas and assessing academic growth, classroom teachers become leaders and champions for the whole child. They do this by teaching and learning in the social and emotional arenas as well. Just as we cannot separate teaching and learning, we can no longer afford to separate academic, social, and emotional learning for teachers and students. These ideas go together.

The real work of the classroom teacher is to systematically care about students and teach students the knowledge and skills that they will need to be successful in the next phase of life. Different ideas about the fundamental purpose of schools have clouded our vision and become a barrier to the progress and human development that we all want to see. We must get back to seeing our students as humans, which requires that we return to the belief that it is the teacher's job to teach the whole child. This means finding a balance and teaching both academic and social-emotional competencies (Weissberg & Cascarino, 2013). This worldview is essential to the real work of the classroom. The classroom teacher cannot limit her work to developing the organ between the ears. The teacher must also teach and learn social-emotional competencies that will enable people to apply cognitive academic knowledge to the problems of our world.

What Is Social and Emotional Learning?

Social and emotional learning (SEL) includes the human knowledge, skills, attitudes, and behaviors that enable us to find success and happiness at home and in the workplace. Aspects of both affective and cognitive domains of learning can be included in the broader definition. In other words, SEL is necessary for both personal and profes-

A Mindfulness Framework

sional growth and achievement. For students, SEL is necessary for individual academic success and a positive classroom community and school climate. The leading research group in SEL, the Collaborative for Academic, Social, and Emotional Learning (CASEL, 2018d), defined SEL in this way:

> Social and emotional learning (SEL) is the process through which children and adults acquire and effectively apply the knowledge, attitudes, and skills necessary to understand and manage emotions, set and achieve positive goals, feel and show empathy for others, establish and maintain positive relationships, and make responsible decisions. (para. 1)

Whether you have learned about SEL or not, you can always know more. You can learn more about your own social and emotional development, and you can learn more about how to teach social-emotional competencies to your students. The field of knowledge for SEL in classrooms and schools has blossomed. Although we have made great progress in this field, there is still much to know and infinite ways to apply the knowledge.

A Little History

The term *social and emotional learning* was first used in 1994 at a meeting hosted by the Fetzer Institute (CASEL, 2018c). This meeting started the formal version of the ongoing conversation about teaching the whole child. In the same year, CASEL was formed. This organization has laid the foundation in the field of SEL research. In collaboration with the Association for Supervision and Curriculum Development (ASCD), CASEL created some of the first SEL resources for educators (CASEL, 2005, 2013; Elias et al., 1997). This work paved the way for teachers to use SEL research in their classrooms in a systematic way. It is on the shoulders of these and other giants that we stand. Today, our aim is twofold: (1) build on the foundation that these researchers have laid and (2) join their cause.

In 2015, CASEL published a comprehensive handbook of the most recent and relevant research in the field (Durlak, Domitrovich, Weissberg, & Gullotta, 2015). One significant insight from the authors' work is that SEL can be taught in various ways and in many contexts (i.e., there is no one, right way). As a classroom teacher, you should feel empowered to use the existing research and resources in a way that supports your professional growth and learning. You should feel empowered to use your professional and ethical judgment to determine which resources will meet the needs of your current learners at the current time. Find what will work and use it.

My hope is that this book will serve as a useful resource to you, adding to the work that already exists. As you read, keep this truth in mind: There is no silver bullet in teaching. Teachers need a large collection of tools at their disposal. Let us build our toolbox together.

A Closer Look: SEL Deconstructed

Social and emotional learning is so many things. Ultimately, when we are teaching students how to be more competent in these areas, we are teaching and modeling practices such as how to get along with others, how to recognize personal and community needs, how to build relationships, and how to be compassionate. There are many impacts of social and emotional learning, including improved academic performance with as much as an 11-percentile gain in achievement (Durlak, Weissberg, Dymnicki, Taylor, & Schellinger, 2011).

SEL focuses on developing humans who are socially aware. Students with self-awareness can recognize their own strengths and areas of need. Self-awareness means knowing what areas you excel in and owning that efficacy. Self-awareness also translates into academic confidence and academic success (Denham & Brown, 2010; Zins, Bloodworth, Weissberg, & Walberg, 2007). Socially aware humans can read others, understanding the needs and emotions of others and responding to them appropriately. One main quality of a socially aware individual is empathy. Socially aware individuals are kind, increasing the kindness quotient wherever they go.

A Mindfulness Framework

Beyond developing these personal and relational qualities, SEL helps kids and adults make good decisions. SEL promotes good behaviors; in other words, "goodness" can be taught and learned. This means that, like academic excellence, social-emotional competence is not innate. We can show others how to be responsible citizens who are productive members of society. We can increase the level of goodness in the world as people learn good behaviors, one socially and emotionally competent student at a time. Like academic excellence and expertise, SEL is a lifelong process that we must pursue for ourselves and expect for our students.

This is a job that is easy to talk about and hard to do. As already mentioned, there are so many ways to teach and learn these necessary life skills. Where do we start, and what skills are most important to learn? If SEL really is about making good people, how do we teach goodness? How do we model good decision making? How do we teach students about being good to themselves and others?

Five Core Competencies

There are many ways to organize how we think about SEL and what should be prioritized for teaching purposes. Rather than get caught up in the taxonomy of SEL competencies, I respectfully defer to the widely researched and accepted resource from CASEL (2018b), the list of the five core SEL competencies: self-awareness, self-regulation, social awareness, relationship skills, and responsible decision making (see Figure 2).

Within the five categories of social-emotional competence, there are many attitudes, skills, behaviors, and conceptual knowledge that can be taught and must be learned throughout one's lifetime. For our purposes, I will address just a few of these ideas:

» **Self-awareness.** Teachers may work with students to develop their abilities to identify their emotions and strengths and develop their self-efficacy in an academic area.

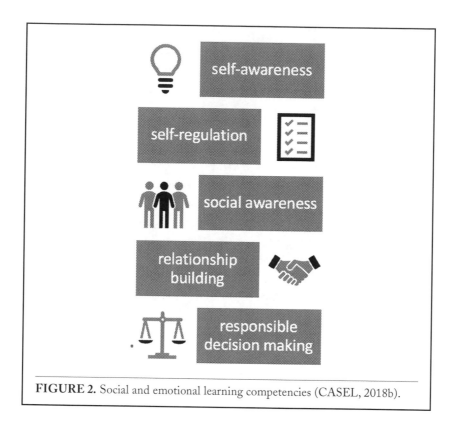

FIGURE 2. Social and emotional learning competencies (CASEL, 2018b).

- » **Self-regulation.** Teachers may support students in self-management by teaching them to set goals or by teaching and assessing certain organizational strategies.
- » **Social awareness.** Teachers may teach students to recognize and respond to the needs of others with compassion.
- » **Relationship skills.** Teachers may work with students on developing empathy while communicating in a team setting.
- » **Responsible decision making.** Teachers might use and teach a model of problem solving or use a set of ethical standards in their classrooms.

The purpose of this text is not to duplicate or replicate the outstanding work that currently exists, but to build upon it, offering up another framework of principles for mindfully attending to the teach-

A Mindfulness Framework

ing and learning of SEL in the classroom. As you can tell, this is a complicated teaching issue. Whatever the approach, the end goal for students is both academic competence and social-emotional competence, resulting in humans who are prepared to solve the complex social, environmental, and political issues of our day.

Ultimately, if we shift our focus to developing SEL competencies in individuals, we should expect increased academic achievements and other benefits as well. When people are socially and emotionally competent, they behave with compassion and seek to raise social consciousness in others.

SEL supports *transformational learning*, or learning that improves the lives of students and the world. This kind of learning is being embraced globally, as institutions of higher education train students to focus on global issues, encouraging crosscultural analysis and collaboration in response to issues of oppression, economic inequity, and social change. Rennick (2015) advocated for a refocus on pedagogical priorities, revisiting the groundbreaking and foundational work of John Dewey, Paulo Freire, and Jack Mezirow. Rennick noted that all three of these innovators supported teaching and learning that honored the student and "can change the mind of the learner and, as a result, make a positive difference in the society in which the learner lives" (p. 73).

A Proposal for Promoting SEL

Let us consider how a mindfulness framework might contribute to the field of social and emotional learning.

- » **Consider the culture of our education system today.** Where do we spend our time, attention, and resources?
- » **Reflect on the gaps in opportunity.** Look at the chasm between what we espouse and what we do. Our values and our actions don't always align. Why not? This is an essential issue. We can address this issue when school leaders and classroom teachers start paying attention.

» **Refocus attention to the whole child.** Since the 1930s, teachers have shared the philosophy of teacher pioneer Ruth Mary Weeks, advocating the need to teach the whole child. Weeks's (1931) voice still resounds as we consider how we can teach children "the elements needed for a complete, happy, and effective life" (p. 110). Let us reembrace Weeks's ideas about preparing children to live and enjoy life, something she calls "the art of living" (p. 112). Let us pay attention to our role in the real and whole life of a person.

» **Focus on our diverse learners.** Even culturally relevant practices fall short when mindfulness is absent. Tom Griggs and Deborah Tidwell (2015) made a case for using mindfulness in teaching and teacher preparation. Their self-study explained the benefits of mindfulness for their teaching practice, especially when navigating the complex world of teaching about multicultural education. Using mindfulness, Griggs and Tidwell made the important distinction between teaching for diversity and teaching in diversity. Without mindful attention to our multicultural selves and our diverse learning environments, teachers will not know when and how to meet the needs of the diverse learners they serve.

» **Pay attention.** This is the first step to mindful practices that promote SEL in the classroom. It is a step toward equitable practice. Because mindfulness encourages equity in a fresh and personal way, it may be the key that will open hearts and change minds.

Mindfulness matters. Mindfulness empowers, motivates, and provides many healthful benefits (Brown, Ryan, & Creswell, 2007). Mindful work gives teachers authority. As the classroom teacher leans into this mindful work with and for her students, she is able to do what is best for kids and for the world. Mindfulness allows teachers to recognize their position as professional change agents. Teachers need mindfulness, and we need teachers to create a mindful movement toward SEL. After all, "teachers are the engine that drives SEL programs and practices in schools and classrooms" (Schonert-Reichl, 2017, p. 137). Let us then begin this work together with teachers, taking one step forward toward equity and transformation.

In summary, I propose that teachers use a mindfulness framework to teach and develop SEL competencies in a systematic and transferrable way. This framework for mindfulness consists of eight principles. Each principle supports the development of one or more SEL competencies. The beauty of this proposal is that it is not an additional program or set of tasks that you must add to an overburdened calendar. The principles can be implemented using simple activities that complement or improve your existing curriculum and classroom management plans. This proposal is practical and accessible to everyone—the novice and master teacher alike.

> *I propose that teachers use a **mindfulness framework** to teach and develop **SEL competencies** in a systematic and transferrable way. This framework for mindfulness consists of **eight principles**. Each principle supports the development of one or more SEL competencies.*

The Eight Mindful Principles: An Overview

The following are the eight mindful principles (see Figure 3) to support the development of social and emotional learning.

Principle 1: "I" Work

The first principle is *"I" work*, which refers to *Identity, Integrity,* and *Inspiration*. "I" work insists on integrity of identity for teachers and students.

Research-based teaching methods and motivations are essential to teacher effectiveness, but they are not enough. "I" work encourages teachers and students to understand their strengths and growth needs,

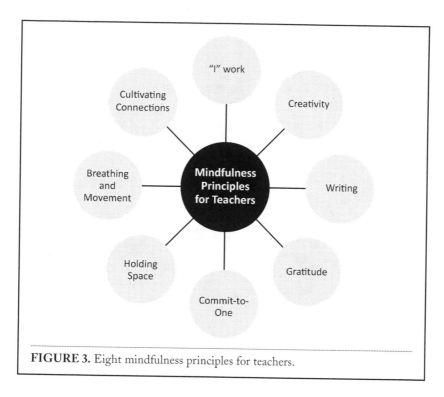

FIGURE 3. Eight mindfulness principles for teachers.

bringing their gifts together for positive change. "I" work is motivated by the "why," "how," "what" model of inspiration (Sinek, 2009). Using this "golden circle," teachers are encouraged to find their "why" (see Figure 4).

"I" work is critical. It is the foundation for the other principles. When teachers have personal and professional integrity of identity, they can lean into the work. Parker Palmer (1998) reminded us that "good teaching comes from the identity and integrity of the teacher" (p. 10). The practice of "I" work gives teachers both ownership and authority to do what is best for students in the classroom.

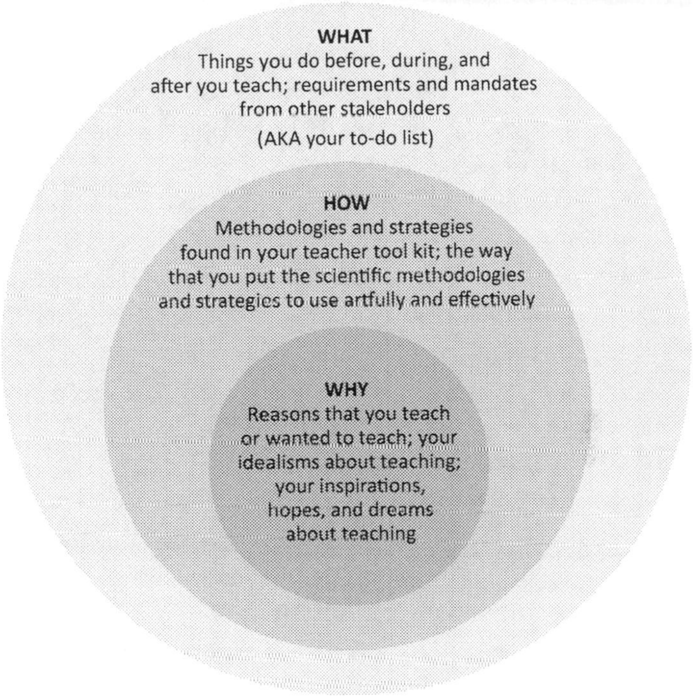

FIGURE 4. The golden circle of teaching (Sinek, 2009).

TRY THIS: Why Teach?—A Think-Pair-Share

Reflect on the reason you went into teaching. Why did you want to teach? Write down your reason and share it with a friend. The statement that you wrote is your "why" statement. Identifying your teaching strengths and gifts often begins with identifying your "why." Your "why" can be your inspiration and the motivation to keep teaching on the most challenging days. Knowing your "why" reminds you of who you are and helps you maintain integrity when the challenging realities of working in schools manifest. Your "why" is at the heart of "I" work.

Principle 2: Creativity

The second principle is *creativity*. We are born creative. Unfortunately, as we learned from Sir Ken Robinson (2006), schools may be the culprit in creativity's demise. Let us stop this trend. Let us not stifle our innate ability or desire to create.

Creating is the highest and final level in the revised version of Bloom's taxonomy of thinking (Krathwohl, 2002). Creating, a mental act of creativity, can inspire us to contribute to our world in unique and profitable ways. Creating results in new, whole, coherent, or original products.

There has never been a more critical time to be creative in the classroom. Creativity helps us connect to ourselves and others in this world. Educators can use the research-based science of teaching and learning in creative ways to meet the needs of their learners. There is an art to mastering effective teaching practice. Kenneth Moore (2015) described teaching using the metaphor of teachers as artists. I love this idea. Thinking of teachers in this capacity reminds us of the need to foster creative thinking in ourselves and our students. Teachers benefit from practicing creativity. Applying this principle grants teachers the creative license to teach as professionals and to be the decision makers in their classrooms. Creativity is a powerful force for teachers and students and for the development of SEL.

Principle 3: Cultivating Connections

The third principle is *cultivating connections*. We do not live in a bubble. Our relationships have a ripple effect, and we never know where our influence stops. Let us learn how to connect with one another beyond social media. Let us relearn how to smile and make eye contact. Let us practice how to build deep and meaningful relationships with those who are similar to and different from ourselves. Cultivating connections is about increasing social capital and the social networks that lead to positive educational change. Cultivating connections is also about finding unity in the populations that we serve.

A Mindfulness Framework

Several relationship essentials, including humility, gentleness, patience, compassion, empathy, peace, and love, apply to classroom contexts. These essentials support effective communication.

Principle 4: Writing

The fourth principle is *writing*. Zinsser (1990) said that writing is thinking. Writing is a creative process that must be taught, practiced, nurtured, and developed. In this principle, writing can be used to develop efficacy in specific content areas (e.g., science, mathematics, social justice, etc.). Writing as mindfulness draws attention to the thought language cycle of learning. It is a natural metacognitive tool and an effective tool for instruction (Bransford, Brown, & Cocking, 2000).

Principle 5: Breathing and Movement

Breathing and movement is the fifth principle. The mind-body connection cannot be ignored. There is a physiological component to all that we do, and we can mindfully use our breath and movement to support SEL in many ways. Breathing and moving are essential to life and essential to improving the quality of life through SEL. Incorporating breathing and movement offers a unique pathway toward mindfulness in schools. Conscious breathing and strategic movement allow opportunities for meditating on learning.

Principle 6: Gratitude

The sixth principle is *gratitude*. We should constantly be in a posture of thanksgiving. Give thanks in good and bad times, celebrating the good and learning from the bad. This principle explores situating gratitude at the heart of everything that we do. Gratitude is a foundation for mindfulness, as it allows us to live in the moment and see opportunities in every situation. Gratitude is both a habit of mind and a practice. There are many simple actions that allow both teachers and students to live more gratefully.

Principle 7: Holding Space

The seventh principle is *holding space*. Holding space involves setting up an environment that allows for mindfulness work to happen. When we hold space, we cultivate both physical and mental space for ourselves and others, taking on the role of facilitator and giving students ownership and authority over their own learning and lives. Holding space supports a culture of mindfulness for all and helps to create intentional learning environments.

Principle 8: Commit-to-One

The final principle is called *commit-to-one*. This principle requires courage. Commit-to-one is about the process of goal setting and commitment-making. It is about turning abstract ideas into concrete plans and taking the first step toward success. Self-awareness, reflection, and regulation are essential parts of this process.

In Summary

So, there you have it, the building blocks for change: five competencies, eight principles, and a proposal. All that's left is to put them together in a way that promotes positive change for individuals, schools, and communities. The remainder of this book is written for that purpose.

Dive into Part II of the book for a deeper discussion and breakdown of the essential ideas of each of the eight principles. For each principle, I have designed some simple and effective activities linking theory to the practice. Enjoy the journey.

A Mindfulness Framework

Discussion Questions

1. In this chapter, we celebrated the teacher as leader and champion. In what ways are you a leader on your campus? In what ways are you a champion?

2. Consider the separate concepts of mindfulness and equity. Using your own professional and personal experience, describe what each of those terms means to you. What is the role of each in our school system? Now, consider these ideas together. How might mindfulness and equity be related? How might one support the other?

3. After reading an overview of the eight principles, which one resonates the most with you, and why? Which one seems most applicable to the work that you currently do in the classroom? Which one would you like to explore further?

Journal Prompt

In this chapter, I wrote about "inserting the lever of change." Consider your sphere of influence. Where could you insert the lever? If you could change one thing in the sphere of where you live and work, what would you change? Imagine the far-reaching implications of this change. What are some steps that you could take to get started? What is the role of social and emotional competence in initiating and completing this change project?

PART II

The Eight Principles

I love those who can smile in trouble, who can gather strength from distress, and grow brave by reflection. 'Tis the business of little minds to shrink, but they whose heart is firm, and whose conscience approves their conduct, will pursue their principles unto death.

—Leonardo da Vinci

There are three constants in life . . . change, choice, and principles.

—Steven Covey

A Story of Principle

My best friend called me recently and told me a story that I will never forget. Through tears of joy, she described an event that she had witnessed one morning as she walked her daughter, River, into her preschool. As they approached the building, she noticed that her

 DOI: 10.4324/9781003236665-5

daughter's pace slowed. River's attention was focused on Chance, a friend from class, who was having a rough start to his day. He was crying. He did not want to go to school or leave the safety and warmth of his dad's arms. River clearly felt the sorrow from Chance. She shared his pain and anguish. Her 5-year-old heart was prompted to act.

My friend gave River the gentle encouragement that she needed. River approached Chance with confidence, courage, and kindness. She asked, "Would you like to walk in with me today?" Chance smiled. A wave of joy and relief washed over everyone watching. He took River's hand. Together, they entered their classroom, ready for a day of learning and fun.

I love this story. I am so grateful to my friend for sharing. This story is an example of living out your principles. River's response to Chance's sadness is a perfect example of empathy. Her mom's response, also empathetic, reveals this family's commitment to noticing and connecting with people.

How many of us would notice a stranger's sadness? How many of us would be brave and respond in a simple, kind, and effective way? River had empathy for Chance. It was a natural feeling. With the guidance of her mom's steady presence, she was encouraged to practice a principled response. The level of humanity was elevated because of her.

River did not act alone—children seldom do. River's mom, an astute observer of her child, was mindful of the situation. She, too, was empathetic, aware of River's feelings, and intent to act. As a nurturing adult, my friend acted with integrity and encouraged River to step out in faith and principle.

There was risk of rejection or humiliation; there always is. But in this case, as it usually is when we follow our principles, the reward was worth the risk. My friend, River, Chance, and anyone watching learned something from this interaction. We can all learn something. This story is a powerful testimony of what is possible when principles of mindfulness and social-emotional learning connect.

It's About Love

River's story is about love. Love is a powerful force in humanity and in this world. Love is an opposing force to exploitation, fear, and hate (Ryoo, Crawford, Moreno, & McLaren, 2009). Love is the critical factor in relationships and connections between individuals. In the field of critical spiritual pedagogy, love, integrity, and power are ways to reclaim humanity (Ryoo et al., 2009). It is through unconditional love that we can begin to relate to one another and understand one another in classrooms, schools, and societies. Paulo Freire (2000) talked about education as an act of love. I tend to agree with Freire and share his hope that education could create a world where it is easier to love. Are we creating this world today?

As I try to make sense of yet another school shooting (Newman, Fox, Roth, Mehta, & Harding, 2005; Williams, Blankstein, Dienst, & Siemaszko, 2018), I wonder, worry, and hope. As a teacher, one of the most important beliefs that sustains my work is hope. Despite some evidence to the contrary, I still believe and hope that education will make a difference. I believe and hope that education and schools can be spaces where it is easier to love.

Teachers can model unconditional love toward their students. Students can love one another. Parents and communities can love the school. We can utilize the relationships that occur in the school setting to promote loving contexts. Freire's (2000) view of education as an act of love lives on today. It lives in us and through us, but only when we practice a principled way of loving one another, as we "do school" together.

Many people find this work puzzling. You might, too. There are many pieces. It is often left to the classroom teacher to see how they fit together. My hope is that in reading this text, you will start to see the puzzle complete.

Puzzle Piece #1

The first puzzle piece is one we know much about: *social and emotional learning*. SEL is important. Beyond general happiness, SEL supports people as they work to relate to one another. In creative contexts, SEL supports collaboration, empathy, and acceptance. It helps people understand who they are and how they fit into the big picture. SEL helps people see why they need to learn and why learning matters. SEL empowers individuals to be themselves and contribute to group success. It gives people value and positive self-concept. When SEL is used in schools, students see themselves as valuable contributors and cocreators of knowledge. Compassion, gratitude, and commitment are shared in positive learning spaces.

SEL competencies enable you to function successfully in society. The business world calls these *soft skills*, which include communication, personal development, and relationship skills. In education, we have boiled this body of learning down into five categories: self-awareness, self-regulation, social awareness, relationship skills, and responsible decision making (CASEL, 2018d). We can look at these as categories of competence needed to be successful. And, yes, there is research that connects competencies in SEL to increased academic performance (Durlak et al., 2011, 2015).

This research points to a simple fact: If we want our students to be successful, we must teach the whole child. Research indicates that it is not only the child who needs support in the development of SEL competencies; teachers also need SEL (Schonert-Reichl, 2017). When teachers develop social and emotional competency in themselves, it is possible for them to support this learning in students. It is also possible to create a positive classroom climate. Thus, these three areas are critical to the success of any SEL program in a school or district: (1) SEL in teachers, (2) SEL in students, and (3) a positive learning environment.

The Eight Principles

Puzzle Piece #2

The second puzzle piece is the *how* piece. How does one go about incorporating activities and finding time to teach SEL competencies in the already overburdened schedule of the school day? The answer is to embed opportunities and activities that teach SEL into the academic teaching and learning that is already occurring. There is time if you do this carefully and mindfully.

So, how does one go about embedding social and emotional teaching and learning? Well, as we have already discussed, there are many ways to do this successfully. One suggestion is the mindfulness framework composed of eight principles offered in this book. In Part II of this book, each principle is deconstructed into its essential parts.

Puzzle Pieces #3 and #4

The third and fourth puzzle pieces are related, both stemming from your teaching practice itself. In the next eight chapters, you will find more than just a theoretical idea of how to apply each principle to your work in the classroom. You will find multiple activities to try, lesson plans, discussion questions, and journal prompts. If you use these practical tools, you will find yourself practicing the principles quickly. It is important to practice the mindfulness principles as you are also teaching your subject matter using effective pedagogies. Combining subject matter expertise (Puzzle Piece #3) and pedagogical expertise (Puzzle Piece #4) within the mindful framework will give you a complete picture and yield both SEL and the academic results you are aiming toward (see Figure 5).

Now that you have the pieces, you can apply your own teaching experience, subject matter expertise, and individual strengths to complete the puzzle. Enjoy the process. A masterpiece awaits.

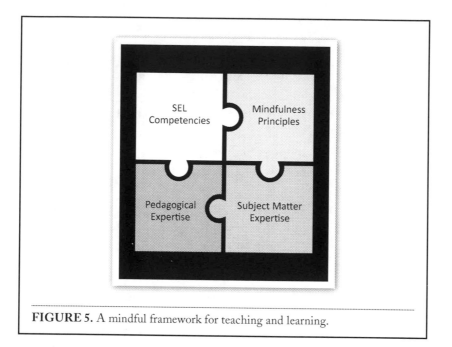

FIGURE 5. A mindful framework for teaching and learning.

"I" Work

In the social jungle of human existence, there is no feeling of being alive without a sense of identity.

—Erik Erikson

The greatness of a man is not in how much wealth he acquires, but in his integrity and his ability to affect those around him positively.

—Bob Marley

During my first year as a teacher educator, I attended a conference in Corpus Christi, TX. I remember being so nervous and feeling completely out of my element. I mean, I could stand up and talk to kids all day long. But now I was talking to adults: my peers, my mentors, my heroes. What could I possibly bring to the table that they didn't already know?

In order to get my mind off of the presentation that I would make later that day, I did something unusual. Instead of attending the morning session that was safe and predictable, the one in my area of research, I chose a different session just because it sounded interesting. I didn't know what the content would be, but something about the title made my heart jump and beat a little faster. Do you know what I am talking about? This is the feeling you get when you find yourself where you are meant to be. It is a feeling of knowing; you are in your element, and you are supposed to be there. In these moments, you can be you. Without shame, you can dream about your potential, the best version of yourself.

I didn't know it at the time, but in that moment, I was learning a lesson in integrity. I found myself being honest and participating in the conversation in a way that made sense to me. All of my original fear and doubt melted away, and the result was fruitful. In that moment, a seed was planted in my heart—the right seed in the right soil at the right time. It would take years to germinate, grow, and bloom, but now, 12 years later, I am writing about it. That is what happens when you have integrity of identity: growth and fruit.

Imagine going to work every day and getting to be yourself—your whole self with no apologies. For some of us, that means telling goofy jokes, bringing a lighthearted mood to the room. For others, it means a stern focus and unyielding sense of duty. Being yourself might mean using music in your classroom, teaching science with poetry, or wearing your favorite tennis shoes because even though you teach French, you are really a runner, and you just can't sit still. Think of what "it" is that makes you, you. Imagine taking that quality with you and using it to inspire yourself and others. Imagine being honest about who you are and how you see the world. Consider allowing your students the same grace. This is the essence of the first principle, called *"I" work*, and it is the connection between *identity, integrity,* and *inspiration.*

"I" work is critical. It is the foundation for the seven principles that follow. When teachers have personal and professional integrity of identity, they can lean into their work. This practice gives them both ownership and authority to do what is best for kids in the classroom. "I" work is about knowing who you are and how your contributions matter. It is about building on strengths and learning while staying true to your values and ideals.

"I" Work

I find inspiration in the mere existence of a person of integrity. Think of a person you know who you might imagine does the right thing even when no one is looking. Think of a person who applies his or her natural and learned gifts selflessly in ways that benefit others. Often, these people make challenging tasks appear effortless. They seem to be doing what they were born to do. They radiate with energy, life, and positivity. Their greatness comes from an understanding of their ability to truly do the best that they can and to help others do the same. We often aspire to be like these individuals, desiring their confidence and ability. The key to getting there is doing the "I" work: becoming more self-aware by learning and capitalizing on your strengths, becoming more socially aware by tuning in to how your strengths may benefit others, and making responsible decisions by using your strengths to meet the needs of other humans or to address issues in your organization as you are able. "I" work supports every category of social and emotional learning for both teachers and students in schools. But it starts with you.

Your Real Work

I love the saying "What you do instead of work is your real work" because it gives you permission to be you. Think about what you do instead of work. What distracts you? What inspires you? What activity causes you to lose all track of time? Knowing this enables you to teach and lead with integrity. One goal of "I" work is to discover your real work and where it aligns with your schoolwork. This is where the magic happens.

TRY THIS: A Credo

Take some time to write your credo for the year. A credo is a statement of beliefs that drive action. Your credo should read like a personal mission statement or series of belief statements that you will use to inform your work.

Steps for writing your credo:
1. Start with personal affirmations: I am _____ . (I am kind. I am smart. I am loving. I am a mother.)
2. Now, write down five things that you believe: I believe _____ .
3. Add a poem, quote, song lyric, or verse that represents you and your beliefs.

Remaining true to yourself and your values is critical in the work of teaching and learning. For many, the key to teacher effectiveness is relationships. The student-teacher relationship is a powerful force and factor in learning. The student-teacher relationship is dynamic. We know that the quality of the student-teacher relationship matters in social and academic outcomes (Hughes, Cavell, & Wilson, 2001). We also know that these relationships begin with the teacher. Because of the obvious and natural power differential between students and teachers, the teacher bears much responsibility in cultivating a culture in which healthy student-teacher relationships form. This requires work.

"I" work insists on integrity of identity for teachers. The three essentials in "I" work—integrity, identity, and inspiration—are discussed in the sections that follow.

Essential #1: Integrity—Be True, Be You

There is a Proverb that says, "The integrity of the upright guides them; But the unfaithful are destroyed by their duplicity" (Proverbs 11:3, New International Version). Integrity is a quality of honesty, moral character, and principle. You cannot be a person of integrity if you consistently lie about who you are and the gifts you bring. Integrity is an essential trait of effective leaders. A leader with integrity inspires his or her followers to maintain their integrity. Therefore, a teacher with integrity teaches her students how to have integrity, too.

Integrity is more than honesty. In work, a person with integrity does his or her work competently and completely, finishing a task and doing what is right even when no one is looking. Are you a person of integrity?

TRY THIS: Simple Integrity Test

List 3–5 values, beliefs, or ideas that you hold dear to your heart. Provide a recent example of how you expressed each value on your list. Reflect on how your life represents the values that you espouse. In which areas can you improve?

A person of integrity fits his or her work into the larger picture of purpose and stays faithful to the vision of the organization. Of course, it helps when that person works in an organization that also has integrity. How can we mindfully determine if an organization has integrity?

TRY THIS: The "Theory of Action" Test for Your Organizations

Step 1: Find a friend or colleague you trust who also knows the organization well and is willing to speak honestly. If possible, choose someone who genuinely cares about the future of the organization. Engage that person in a dialogue about integrity. Ask him or her to join you in an exploration of your organization's theory of action (Argyris, 1997), a litmus test for integrity. (A word of caution: Avoid the temptation to vent or complain during this step; this conversation is meant to be instructive and constructive.)

Step 2: Locate and read your organization's mission and vision statement. If the organization does not have one, stop here. Gather the proper team and write one.

Step 3: Analyze the statement. What does it say that your organization does? Make a list or a graphic organizer that charts the qualities and values of your organization.

Step 4: Ask yourself: *Are we doing what we say we are doing?* Reflect on the practices that you know happen consistently in your organization. Consider who leads the activities and how many members participate. Compare this list with the list of espoused qualities that you determined in Step 3. Begin to align the espoused and enacted values. Notice the gaps.

Step 5: Dig deeper. Take a vision walk around campus. Look for other evidence that your organization is meeting the published goals and mission. You may not know all of the wonderful things that are happening. Take notes. Talk to other members to ask them how they complete or fulfill their roles in the overall function of the organization. (*Note.* This analysis is meant to examine your organization as a whole. It is not meant to be a "gotcha" for any one individual. If you talk to people, please do so mindfully, with grace and forgiveness, inviting them into the conversation.)

Step 6: Make a final analysis. Individually or with your partner, consider the following: In which areas is your organization fulfilling its mission and vision? What are you doing well? What specific things are done to make sure the core values of the institution are being protected? In which areas is the organization falling short? Brainstorm possible solutions to any identified issues.

Step 7: Reflect. Based on your findings, is there a culture of integrity at your institution? Are you doing what you say you are doing? Do you enact what you espouse? If not, what are some things in your sphere of influence that you can do to address the shortcomings? If the organization is fulfilling its mission and has a culture of integrity, congratulations! Keep up the great work. And buy your campus leader some flowers.

Integrity in the Classroom

Although we can hope that integrity is modeled and learned in most homes, we cannot assume that this is the case. The good news is that integrity can be taught, and the classroom is a wonderful place to ensure that this is happening. Integrity is a necessary quality for achieving social and emotional competency in the areas of relationships and responsible decision making. So how do you introduce the concept of integrity to your students in a mindful way?

First, it is essential to define integrity in a kid-friendly way. My favorite definition of integrity is: *what you do when no one else is watching*. Consider using a Frayer model (Frayer, Frederick, & Klausmeier, 1969) to explicitly teach this term (see Figure 6).

Other powerful vocabulary instructional strategies could also work. Perhaps you could create a "Mindful Word Wall" by designating a bulletin board to display all of the vocabulary that you are teaching and using related to mindfulness and SEL. This bulletin board could also serve as a place to celebrate and publish students' mindful acts by posting written narratives or photographs of real student behavior as examples under each term on the word wall. Whatever strategy you choose, teach SEL and mindfulness terms explicitly whenever possible; if these ideas are not defined, they can often seem subjective, left to individual interpretation. We want to be clear and ensure that students know that these concepts have meaning. The meanings will matter greatly as students attempt to apply these ideas in their lives. See Table 2 for a list of student-friendly vocabulary definitions.

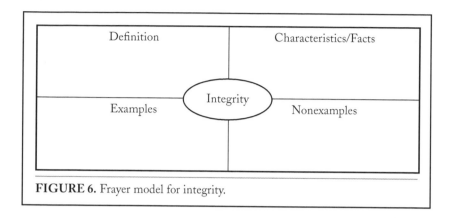

FIGURE 6. Frayer model for integrity.

TRY THIS: Create a Concept Cube

Create a paper cube or use a model like the one pictured below to teach various SEL vocabulary words. Work with students to decorate each side with the following information:

- Vocabulary word
- Synonym
- Antonym
- Definition
- Example sentence
- Picture

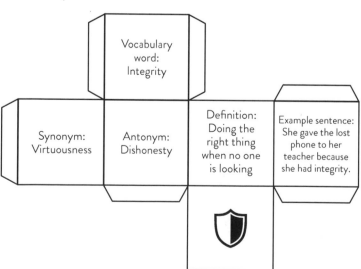

"I" Work

TABLE 2

Mindfulness and SEL Vocabulary for Kids

Words	Student-Friendly Definitions	Examples
Academic success	Doing well in school; learning	Finishing a project; learning how to do a math problem
Aware, Awareness	Knowing what is going on around you; noticing; seeing	Seeing that someone is sad and sharing with that person
Communication, Communicating	Talking, listening, or writing so that you can share ideas and feelings with others and understand other people	Talking, texting, listening, and reading
Compassion	Being kind to someone when he or she needs a friend; showing someone you care; doing something nice for someone; helping someone	Bringing someone cookies; giving a hug to someone when he is sad; listening to a friend when her feelings are hurt; helping someone if he falls
Competence	Being good at something; being able to do something	Doing a back handspring in gymnastics; reading a book; being able to do your math homework by yourself
Connection	Being friends with someone	Sharing ideas and inside jokes; knowing you are friends with someone
Conscious Breathing	Counting your breaths; paying attention to your breathing	Taking a deep breath before a test
Commit-to-One	Trying something new	Writing something on your calendar to try
Creativity	Making or building something; new ideas	Building with blocks, painting, and writing a story
Efficacy	Believing that you can do it	Having confidence in yourself
Emotions	Feelings	Sadness, happiness, anger, and joy
Empathy	Noticing when your friend feels sad or scared and feeling sad, too	Feeling sad when your friend is sad about her sick puppy

TABLE 2, *continued*

Words	Student-Friendly Definitions	Examples
Gentleness, Gentle	Nice, sweet, calm; softly touching	Softly petting your pet; saying something nice to your friend
Good behavior	Being nice; following directions and listening; obeying adults	Listening to your mom; doing what your teacher says
Gratitude, Grateful	Thanking someone; saying thank you; being thankful and happy	Writing a thank-you note for a gift; feeling thankful when someone helps you
Holding Space	Staying with people while they do their work; helping when others need it	Sitting at a table with someone while that person does their homework; reading a book to your baby brother
Humility	Not bragging; not getting a "big head"	Thanking people who help you win an award
Identity	Who you are; what you like to do; what you are good at	A baseball player, a dancer, a Texan, a member of the debate team, class president, etc.
Inspiration, Inspiring, Inspired	A feeling like you want to do something; being excited to try	You saw a video of kids building a robot and now you want to build a robot
Integrity	Doing the right thing when no one is looking	Finding a phone on the playground and turning it in to the office at school
Kindness, Kind	Being a friend; helping and smiling; being nice to others and treating them how you want to be treated	Helping your grandma carry in her groceries; calling your cousin to tell him happy birthday
Meditation	Focusing; thinking about something really hard	Visualizing hitting the ball in your baseball game; thinking about someone who was kind to you
Mindfulness	Paying attention	Focusing on the people you are talking to; making eye contact

"I" Work

TABLE 2, *continued*

Words	Student-Friendly Definitions	Examples
Movement	Exercising, walking, or using your body	Stretching for 5 minutes; walking around the track
Patience	Waiting without getting mad	Sitting still and waiting until your family is ready to leave for church
Peace	Calm and rest	Being quiet; playing lullabies at night before bed
Social	Being with friends	Riding bikes with your neighbors
Technology	Tools that help us	Computers and phones
Unity	Being together	Our class working together and sharing
Writing	Putting your ideas on paper	Writing a letter or story

Storytelling is another powerful method of teaching SEL. Stories can be used to teach kids about integrity. Once you have defined integrity and shared a story about what that concept means to people in the world, consider letting students experience what it feels like to act with integrity. If it is age-appropriate, you might consider sending students on an "integrity walk." This walk would allow them, either alone or with a partner, to follow the campus rules and procedures without you policing their every move. When they return to the classroom, ask them how it felt to act with integrity. There are many other ideas for exploring the idea of integrity. Be creative and try some of these on your own or with your students.

TRY THIS: Integrity Stories

With students, read and discuss the following story about integrity (Neff, 1989):

> It was the summer of 1989 when 7-year-old Tanner Munsey taught the world a lesson about integrity. During his T-ball game, he caught the ball and attempted to tag a runner out. Much to his surprise, the umpire responded to the runner, "You're out!" But Tanner protested. He knew that he had missed and that the runner was safe. He knew that it wouldn't be fair if the runner were called "out." He couldn't live with the injustice. Tanner acted with integrity.
>
> A few weeks later, a similar thing happened. This time, the umpire said, "Safe!" Tanner shuffled back to his base, visibly deflated. "What's wrong, Tanner?" the umpire asked. Tanner explained to the umpire that he had, in fact, tagged the runner out. Immediately, the umpire yelled, "You're out!" The umpire knew that Tanner was a kid of integrity. Tanner had earned her trust, and he was rewarded. Not only did he get the "out" that day, but his story was also featured in a July 1989 edition of *Sports Illustrated*. When you have integrity, the world takes notice.

TRY THIS: Integrity Interviews (for Teachers or Students)

One excellent tool to analyze the level of integrity that you bring to your work is the integrity interview. In this activity, you will interview others about yourself. Identify 1–2 people with whom you work or go to school and ask them the following:

1. Define integrity and why it is important in schools.

2. When was a time that you saw me doing something good and honest?
3. Is there a time when you remember me admitting that I was wrong or apologizing for something that I did? Tell me about it.
4. Would you describe me as a person of integrity? Why or why not?

Integrity as Wholeness

People of integrity have some qualities that we can all agree on: honesty, honor, decency. But let us consider one more quality and another way to think about and define integrity for teachers and students. As we mindfully develop SEL competencies together, let us consider integrity as a kind of wholeness.

Something that has integrity is whole. When parts are missing or left out, tragedies occur. For example, on a recent flight from New York to Dallas, an airplane experienced a tragedy of integrity when an engine exploded (Stack & Stevens, 2018). Luckily, the plane had two engines. However, when that engine exploded, part of the blade broke a passenger's window, destroying the integrity of the plane. The plane was no longer whole or able to function. The result was a tragic in-air accident, resulting in loss of life and an emergency landing.

Wholeness matters. Just as an airplane without integrity cannot fly, a teacher without integrity cannot teach. What do you need to be whole? What do your students need? What do you need to be able to function with consistency and accuracy? Integrity.

Palmer (1998) talked about the need to find gladness in the work of teaching. The best teachers are glad and find joy in the work that they do. I have been most glad when I have been teaching from a place of wholeness. For me, this means applying all of the knowledge and skills that I have acquired to the planning and execution of my teaching practice. I am most glad when I am acting from a place of integrity. I find joy when I bring my whole self to my work, accessing all aspects of my identity.

Essential #2: Identity—Know Who You Are

Identity is a combination of how we see ourselves in the world and how others see us. It is the core of who we are as humans. It is a complicated concept, studied and theorized to the nth degree. Identity matters in the classroom and is one part of the "I" work that enables teachers to be mindful about how they present themselves in their classrooms. Identity and integrity are knitted together. When you know who you are and what matters to you, you are able to act from a place of wholeness, maintaining integrity at work and play.

Gee (2000) offered a useful deconstruction of the term *identity* as the "kind of person" that you are (p. 99). What kind of person are you? Can you be "you" in any given context? Or does your identity change as you move from home to work?

Integrity of identity ("I" work) is about being your authentic, human self at all times. When you can maintain your core identity, you can remain whole. Bolman and Deal (2001) talked about this concept in their book *Leading With Soul*, in which they discussed gifts of leadership and how reconnecting spirit or soul to the workplace can have profound benefits. What does this have to do with teaching, mindfulness, and SEL, you ask? Everything. Let me explain.

Teachers are leaders in the classroom. They must be the kind of people who see themselves as confident decision makers, able to facilitate the learning business in the classroom. Teachers must be the kind of people who can lead and teach children and interact professionally with colleagues, parents, principals, etc. They must be the kind of people with subject matter expertise that allows them to help novices translate and transfer prior knowledge into new knowledge. They must boldly but gently correct conceptual misunderstandings or misconceptions. Teachers must see themselves as able and, therefore, have efficacy around their teaching practice. Teaching efficacy comes from observing, experiencing, and reflecting on successful (and unsuccessful) classroom events.

Self-efficacy, including teaching efficacy, involves perceptions of ability and can come from a strong sense of identity (Bandura, 1982).

"I" Work

There has been much work done in this area, so let me provide a brief overview of Gee's (2000) contributions.

Overview of Gee's Identity Theory

Gee (2000) stated that there are four ways to think about what "kind of person" someone is. There are:
>> Natural aspects of identity (Nature-identity or N-identity),
>> Institutional-identity (I-identity) informed by position,
>> Discourse-identity (D-identity) powered by dialogue, and
>> Affinity-identity (A-identity) powered by the groups that we join or how we participate in our social networks.

All four ways are interconnected and useful. Gee advocated using this frame for understanding identity in educational research. I suggest using this frame as a way to be mindful in the practice of teaching. When we mindfully consider our own identities, we can develop the persuasive self-talk that will influence both our emotional state and our sense of efficacy. The result is the courage and confidence to try. When we try and succeed, our efficacy increases. When we try and fail, we learn. Or, as my dad would say, "sometimes chickens, sometimes feathers; either way is good."

So, how can we apply this identity theory to our "I" work? First, consider who you are within each domain.
>> You have natural traits, characteristics, and abilities. What are they? Your answers inform your N-identity.
>> What is your formal position within your organization? What other informal roles do you play? Your answers inform your I-identity.
>> With whom do you engage in ongoing dialogue? What is the content of these conversations? What are the outcomes of these conversations (either actions or emotional states)? Your answers inform your D-identity.

» What groups have you joined, or where do you participate in your social networks? What activities or events do you take pride in? Your answers inform your A-identity.

Consider how the answers to these questions collectively influence how you see yourself. Consider how the answers influence the perceptions of others. With an honest assessment, you may begin to recognize strengths and talents that are authentically you. You may also notice areas that need attention. You may guide your students through a similar exploration and/or use these categories to understand your students and their needs for your own purposes.

For example, consider a third-grade student who is the oldest sibling of three. Her age and birth order are part of her N-identity. This third grader learned English as a second language. She is currently labeled "advanced high" in all four language domains: reading, writing, listening, and speaking. Her label as English language learner and her achievement level are part of her I-identity. This third grader's teachers, parents, and peers all see her and talk about her as a leader in the classroom. The conversations with and about her leadership skills are part of her D-identity. Finally, this third grader is a member of the Bibliophile "Book Worm" Club, a group that meets in the library every day before school to read. She is always present at the meetings and can usually be found toting around five books—the library's limit. Her engagement in this club is part of her A-identity.

Of course, there is more to this student than what is described here. However, consider how Gee's (2000) identity framework might be a starting point for a teacher when planning for a student's individual learning needs, especially when it comes to teaching SEL.

Knowing ourselves and our students will allow us to think mindfully about how our identity can be used to support development of SEL competencies. Teachers can use information about students' identities to inform their lesson planning.

"I" Work

TRY THIS: Lesson Planning With "I" Work

Consider the hypothetical third grader's identity (see p. 66) and use it to preplan a lesson on empathy, an important SEL competency for social awareness and building relationships. List the four categories and defining characteristics of each part of her identity. Then, for each category, consider the implications for teaching and some practical applications for teaching empathy. The first two categories have been completed for you. Once you think through each domain and the implications and applications for teaching, write the lesson plan.

Preplanning Notes for Hypothetical Third Grader

N-identity: Oldest sibling of three
- *Implications for Teaching SEL, Empathy:* As an older sibling, this student may have experienced opportunities to care for and consider the needs and feelings of her younger siblings. Therefore, this student likely has some real-life examples of empathy to discuss. If the teacher knows this, the teacher can use this information to discuss family relationships and the necessity for empathy in homes.
- *Practical Application in the Lesson Planning:* With the student, define the term *empathy* using a Frayer model, including examples and nonexamples from her life with her siblings.

I-identity: English language learner, advanced across all domains (reading, writing, listening, speaking)
- *Implications for Teaching SEL, Empathy:* Learning English as a second language must have been challenging. Ask the student, "How did it feel? Who cared, and how did they show that they cared? Who noticed how you might have been feeling as you were learning?" Label this experience as *empathy*.
- *Practical Application in Lesson Planning:* Knowing this information can be important in heterogenous grouping. Give this student an opportunity to show empathy to others as she acts as the more capable peer in her learning group.

Imagine using identity exploration as a tool for planning and differentiating instruction for your students. Although time-consuming, the results would be individualized instruction that would truly support students' understanding of SEL. When you engage in any exploration of students' identities (formal or informal), you are showing that you are the kind of teacher who cares.

Metacognition

Many teachers and scholars have reflected on the notion that "what the teacher knows is less important than who the teacher is." How can a teacher know who he or she is? The answer: metacognition.

Metacognition is the tool used for "thinking about thinking," and it is the ability to "do" and "think" at the same time. It allows you to practice and improve your practice simultaneously. Metacognition is an effective tool for learning that leads to self-efficacy and confidence (Bransford et al., 2000). When used correctly, metacognition becomes that gentle voice of correction, allowing the teacher to try just about anything. There is little risk of failure when the reward is learning. With this kind of growth mindset, teachers can try anything. So, how do you instill metacognition in yourself and your students?

Metacognition can be taught, practiced, and developed to support students as they become more self-aware. Being metacognitive enables students to regulate themselves as they are learning.

TRY THIS: The How-to Assignment

Give students an assignment in class but explain that they will not complete the assignment. Instead, they will discuss with a partner how they *would* complete the assignment. Simple, but not easy. Facilitate a class discussion, allowing students to share how they would complete the assignment. Create a class anchor chart with the steps required to complete the assignment.

"I" Work

Debrief the activity with students. Tell them that what they have just done is a kind of thinking called *metacognition*. Explain that metacognition is thinking about an assignment and determining steps that you will take before completing the task. It is intentionally thinking about the learning task. Metacognition can lead to higher performance, better grades, less frustration, and more learning.

If possible, add the word *metacognition* to your classroom's mindful word wall. Consider posting the anchor chart that you just completed as the example. Encourage your students to use metacognition on future assignments. Tell students that they don't always have to write down their steps. Thinking about the steps that they will take works too.

Essential #3: Inspiration— Motivate Others and Yourself

If you cannot bring your whole self to work, your light will fade, and you will lose the ability to inspire yourself and others. Inspiration is a key aspect of human motivation, both intrinsic and extrinsic. If you can inspire yourself, you can inspire others. Inspiration, the breathing in of life, requires energy—energy that should not be wasted putting on a facade every morning when you walk into the classroom. Why do you think that scripted curricula are rarely received with enthusiasm?

Teachers are artists, crafting their lessons to match both their students' needs and their own unique creative strengths. Teachers must be given creative license. For this reason, it is essential for teachers to know who they are and stay true to themselves. The same is true for students. Once the teacher and the students know who they are and how they are staying truthful to that message, they can begin to inspire themselves and others.

A Note on Mindfulness and Equity

Critical spiritual pedagogy (Ryoo et al., 2009) is about using humanity, power, and spirituality to promote equity. Rather than devalue the identities that students, teachers, and others bring, we mindfully choose to celebrate identities and utilize the strengths found within. The result is empowering individuals in the education context. Mindfulness may be a pathway to the equity that we seek to achieve in our system. What could be more inspiring than that?

In Summary

We are attempting to bring humanity back into the classroom by connecting identity, integrity, and inspiration. Ryoo et al. (2009) called this work "critical spiritual pedagogy." I call this work "I" work. Either way, this work requires mindfulness.

Discussion Questions

1. Define *integrity* in your own words. How are identity and integrity related?
2. Consider your natural, institutional, affinity, and discursive identities. What strengths do you bring to your work?
3. Identify one person who lives a life of integrity of identity. How does this person inspire you?

Journal

This chapter discussed the importance of explicitly teaching vocabulary related to SEL and mindfulness using student-friendly terms (see Table 2). Why is this important?

Creativity

The true sign of intelligence is not knowledge but imagination.
—Albert Einstein

Sir Ken Robinson (2006) posited that schools kill creativity. In schools, we tend to focus on what is going on between the ears, rather than the rest of the body. I'd go even further to say that our "between the ear" mentality is lopsided; we neglect the talents and capacities of the creative side of the brain, instead focusing on analytical activities, such as analyzing data, learning logic, and mathematical problem solving. By doing so, we ignore our students' intuitive, instinctive, and creative talents.

So, what strategies can we implement so that we are teaching with the whole brain in mind (Jensen, 2005)? How do we address this issue mindfully? And how will developing our creative selves support SEL?

Creativity is the second principle in our mindfulness framework. There are many ways to use creativity in both academic and social-emotional learning. In this chapter, we will discuss some essen-

DOI: 10.4324/9781003236665-7

tials to consider when using creativity to mindfully support SEL in the classroom.

Creativity Defined

Creativity has been defined as the ability to create using the imagination (University of Pennsylvania, 2018). Consider all of the ways that we use our imaginations: to drive our artistic endeavors, to creatively solve problems in work and in relationships, and to initiate ideas and dreams to give us a vision for the future. Imagination supports the development of many other necessary skills for success. Because imagination enables us to envision possibilities beyond our present realities, it can inspire, ignite a passion for work and learning, develop critical thinking abilities, and even enable us to persist through trials and adversity. Imagination is a powerful motivating force, essential for survival in the world today. How do we help ourselves and others learn to use our imaginations better?

TRY THIS: The Junk Test

To invent, you need a good imagination and a pile of junk.
—Thomas Edison

Gather a pile of 15–20 random objects. Use these objects to create something new. Invent something—perhaps useful or perhaps not. The purpose is the process, not the product. When you finish, admire your invention. Do not be too critical. Imagine what other objects you would need to improve upon your design. Imagine the possibilities for how you might use this task in a classroom with students. The possibilities are endless.

Creativity

Creativity Affects Behavior

Imagining is a mental act. As a result, unless we have the access, ability, and permission to utilize sophisticated brain-imaging technology, it cannot be observed or measured. However, there are some creative behaviors that are observable. In fact, over time, we can measure improvements in performance behaviors because of the mental act of imagining.

Imagining a physical performance improves a physical performance. There is evidence to support this claim in the areas of balance and strength (Cha & Kim, 2016). If you imagine exercising before you exercise, you will actually be able lift more (Ranganathan, Siemionow, Liu, Sahgal, & Yue, 2004). There is a well-documented connection between the mind and the body (Blakeslee & Blakeslee, 2007). Could imagining and intentional use of the creative imagination improve performance in other areas as well? Let us explore this idea further.

Let us consider what happens when we use our creative imaginations to envision our futures. The research indicates that mental acts, such as imagining our future through personal goal setting does significantly improve academic performance (Yusuff, 2018). Moreover, future-oriented thinking increases behaviors such as persisting in difficult circumstances, attempting challenging tasks, and using new approaches to problem solving (Destin, Vida, & Townsend, 2018). Imagining the future allows one to better manage tasks in the present. These behaviors support self-awareness, self-regulation, and responsible decision making. Therefore, creativity and imagination support the development of social and emotional skills needed for persisting during challenging academic courses and seasons.

TRY THIS: Birthday Goals

When you celebrate your birthday this year, imagine where you will be in one year. What will you have accomplished? What will make you proud? How will you have grown physically, spiritually, and intellectually? Now, working backward from that vision, what must you do to accomplish those feats? Write three birthday goals.

When we help students imagine their futures, they are inspired to work backward, setting goals that will help them reach their destination. Goal setting is motivating and can help students regulate their behaviors and make responsible decisions. As a result, we might begin to see an increase in positive behaviors, such as self-discipline, organization, and diligence.

Essential #1: Creativity Must Be Practiced and Cultivated

Creative thinking is a kind of critical thinking that includes analysis, synthesis, and possibly even evaluation. It can support artistic abilities, but that is not a requirement. Like other types of thinking, creative thinking can be modeled, nurtured, practiced, and developed. In other words, you can teach people how to think creatively, and their abilities can improve over time. Therefore, you can teach creativity. But first, teachers must practice creative thinking for themselves.

Creative problem solving must be practiced. It must be cultivated. In our culture of standardized testing and black-and-white answers, both teachers and students can get frustrated when presented with open-ended problems. Practice decreases frustration. Teachers can also decrease frustration by cultivating a space where creative thinking is honored, respected, rewarded, and even expected.

TRY THIS: Creative Problem Solving

Think of a problem that you are currently experiencing in your classroom. Make a list of the top 3–5 traditional or textbook-approved solutions. Throw your list away.

Now, think: Is there another solution? Is there a way that you could involve others in this problem-solving exercise? How might you solve the problem if you had unlimited resources? What solution might you suggest if you had unlimited time?

Make a new list. Is it better? Great! Throw that list away.

Start again. Go through several iterations of this exercise until you have arrived at a new, outside-of-the-box solution.

Essential #2: Creativity Takes Time

Creativity is a higher order thinking skill (Krathwohl, 2002). Developing the ability to think creatively requires time. We must deliberatively devote time to developing creativity for academic and social-emotional learning.

Students need permission to think creatively about what they are learning (Moore, 2015). They need to see models of creative applications of learned content. They need to see the connection between creativity and content in real and relevant ways. Students need time to imagine what newly learned concepts might mean to them and how they might be applied to their lives. Students need time to process how they feel about the content they are learning. Creativity matters and can be used to increase academic and social-emotional learning.

Creative thinking is a process. A common misconception is that creativity can only be applied in art, music, or dance. That is simply not the case. A creative thinking process can be applied to most disciplines. Consider the use of creativity in any design process, which encourages students to solve problems using a simple backward design approach. Design thinking is creative thinking that can be taught and practiced systematically. It is a thinking process that can be facilitated by the classroom teacher. Let's learn more.

The Design Thinking Process

The following is a brief overview of a design thinking process (Brown, 2009) that you can teach to students and use in many applications:

» Start with the problem. When possible, talk to the people for whom you are providing the solution and seek their input. Develop empathy for them and their needs. Work with them on developing some solutions.

» Do the research. Brainstorm possible solutions. Generate and develop ideas.

» Based on your ideas, build a model or a prototype, or write a plan.

» Develop a way to test your proposed solution. Take copious notes throughout the process. Get feedback from stakeholders and make improvements. Test again.

» Continue the process until you have a viable, working solution.

This detailed, careful process takes time. Although creativity can be applied to life events or everyday routines, it generally takes time to develop or implement a new process.

TRY THIS: Schedule Creative Time

Can you find a time for creativity—daily, weekly, or monthly? Block out some time in your life to think through a problem and find some solutions. Could you use your creative time for future-oriented thinking and goal setting? Let's schedule some time right now:

* **Daily:** Think about your daily schedule. Is there a time of day that you can schedule a time for creative thinking? Get out your planner. Find 10 minutes at the end of your day today when you can reflect on what happened. Imagine making tomorrow better than today. What steps must you take tomorrow to turn your vision into reality? Write them down.

Creativity

- **Weekly:** Pick a day of the week. Circle that day on your calendar. This is your day for creativity. Plan a creative exercise or experience for yourself and do it on this day. Write a poem. Paint a picture. Sing a song. Take a walk and imagine the possibilities for your life. Be creative when thinking of experiences. One of my favorite weekly creative exercises happens in my kitchen. Once a week, on Monday evenings, I try a new recipe or meal. I express my creativity through the culinary arts, enjoying the freedom and excitement of both the process and the product.
- **Monthly:** Schedule a monthly date with creativity. Commit to learning something new each month. Attend a class, read a book or article, or watch a video with a new idea or method to try. Try it.

Essential #3: Creativity Is Inclusive

When we think about creativity as an activity limited to the visual arts, it becomes exclusive. Have you ever heard someone say, "I am not creative; I am not an artist"? This is simply not true. We are all born with the ability to think creatively. Teachers can facilitate this innate ability by teaching creative processes in collaborative contexts (Gibney, 1998).

TRY THIS: Community Collaborative Art Project

Find a learning space that needs to be decorated. Working together with teaching colleagues, find a feasible collaborative art project to fill the space. Get permission from your principal and others as needed. Execute the project, inviting as many stakeholders as possible to join in the creative process. If you can, invite student artists, teacher artists, parent artists, and administrative artists to work together on this project. Invite people who don't think of themselves as artists and have each person create a piece of the project. With your teaching colleagues, collect the individual pieces, and install them into the space, filling in any missing space with your own creations. Some possible ideas for this type of project include painting a mural, making a mosaic, or doing a collaborative dot project. Enjoy both the process and the product of this community effort.

When we mindfully create opportunities for creativity in our lives and in our classrooms, creativity has the potential for promoting equity. Creative communities work together to solve problems. In these experiences, people have opportunities to develop relationships and connections. Creative projects bring diverse communities together, working toward a common goal.

One such example of the way a creative effort can combat inequity in our system is The Preuss School at the University of California, San Diego (Alvarez & Mehan, 2010). I had the unique honor and privilege to teach science to middle and high school students at this school. It was there that I witnessed the possibilities of a community effort toward ending oppression. There are creative policies and practices that can end the systematic inequality that exists in our classrooms and schools, and it is a beautiful thing to see (Mehan, 2012). The Preuss School, designed to provide a college-going culture and prepare first-generation students from low-income backgrounds for higher education, is truly transformative (Kucher, 2012).

Essential #4: Creativity Takes Courage

Creativity is for everyone, but not everyone has had a chance to flex their creative muscles. This is true for both adults and children, especially as they move up the ranks in our academic system. When we think about creative people, we often envision radical artists and inventors (e.g., Salvador Dali, Frida Kahlo, and the Wright brothers). However, the esteem in which we regard "the creative people" might be the pedestal we trip over on the way to becoming creative ourselves. You may not be the next Marie Curie or Stephanie Kwolek (or maybe you are), but you do have the ability to be creative. You just have to find the courage to try.

Creativity takes courage. Courage increases when people are given a chance to try and fail in a safe and nurturing environment. Part of the creative process is developing multiple solutions or ideas, not all of which will succeed. There are multiple stages to this process, and these stages are recursive (Gibney, 1998). The recursive nature of the creative process requires us to muster up our courage time and time again. Let us encourage one another as we try to find our creative selves. Let us grant one another permission to access our innate creativity, even if it means that we fail. Let us encourage one another to be mindful of our creative brains and to find beauty and solutions in the mess of our busy lives.

In Summary

I believe that creative practices can become pathways toward social and emotional competence. As I watch my precious young son and his best buddies create monster truck jumps and ramps from cardboard, salt dough, and a few bottles of old paint, I pray that the schools they will attend cultivate their beautiful, creative minds and hearts. Be the teacher that keeps creativity alive for them and for all of us.

Discussion Questions

1. Do you think that schools are killing creativity? What can you do to stop this trend?
2. Think about a problem that exists in your classroom. How can you use the design thinking process to solve the problem?
3. In this chapter, I asked you to look at your schedule and find time to be creative. Did you? What was the outcome?

Journal Prompt

Think about yourself as a child. What creative activities did you pursue? What did you believe you could do before you started believing that you couldn't? What "killed" your creativity? How can you get it back?

Cultivating Connections

Be completely humble and gentle; be patient, bearing with one another in love.

Make every effort to keep the unity of the Spirit through the bond of peace.

—Ephesians 4:2–3, NIV

No significant learning can take place without a significant relationship.

—James Comer

Connecting With Students

When I was a first-year teacher, my classroom management was *bad*. If this were a joke, you might ask, "How bad was it?" Unfortunately, this is no joke. From my ninth graders' perspective, sitting in chairs was completely optional. Sitting on desks, though, was totally normal. Also, it seemed perfectly acceptable to eat from, drink from, or

 DOI: 10.4324/9781003236665-8

dispose of the laboratory materials regularly, especially prior to the commencement of lab time. When I tried to greet the students at the door, as Harry Wong (Wong & Wong, 2009) suggested, I would walk into a classroom of chaos. There were tears, y'all! So many tears.

One day, in early October, I frantically tried to get the attention of 43 adolescent biology students. I wanted to teach. I had planned the lesson. I had practically earned my Xerox repair license making the copies. I wanted to start class. I was the teacher, and I'd had enough.

I devised an ingenious plan to take on the leader of the student anarchy. I prepared to authoritatively call him out and to flex my teacher muscle. For me, it all came down to that wild and desperate moment when I was finally ready to show my students who was boss.

When I stood to speak, I glared at the student, flipped my ponytail, pointed my 22-year-old finger, and time stood still. My words failed me. I froze, silenced by the sudden and terrible realization that I had absolutely no clue what this student's name was. I sat back down, defeated and humbled in the sudden knowledge that I had completely failed those kiddos.

I had complained for weeks about them. I complained about their behavior and their attitudes. I complained about their talking. I complained that there were so many students talking at once that I couldn't tell who was talking. But that day, I learned the hard way that I didn't know who was talking because I didn't know who they were. I wanted to teach biology. But I didn't want to teach biology to *them* because I didn't know them. I didn't even know their names. It was October. Shame on me.

Although I felt shame then and for a long time afterward, I am able to share this story now with extreme hope and optimism. The purpose of this confession is not to discredit my service; I did eventually learn who my students were, my classroom management improved, and I never made that mistake again. But if I would have known then what I know now, that mistake never would have happened. My hope is that you will know your students. My hope is that you will not make the same mistake that I did. You'll make different ones! But, trust me, it'll be OK.

Cultivating Connections

All levity aside, my worldview changed that year. I learned that I would never teach biology. I would teach students. Occasionally, I would teach students to love biology the way that I do. More often, and most importantly, I would try to teach students that I love them. But before I could teach them anything at all, I would have to learn the lesson that I share with you now: Know thy students.

Know and cultivate relationships with them that will make them better humans. The connections that you build will make you a better human, too—and a better teacher.

The purpose of this chapter is to dive into this idea of connections and to share some essentials that will help you cultivate connections with yourself, your students, and your colleagues. We will start our discussion by talking about self-care and end with a focus on relationships.

Relationships matter. Mindful attention to them will promote social and emotional learning in your classroom. If you commit to implementing these concepts into your world, I promise that you will see positive outcomes in the lives of the people you serve. You will see positive outcomes for yourself. You will see greater intellectual engagement and more learning. And, for any desperate first-year teachers out there, your classroom management will improve.

Social Capital 101

When we talk about making connections and building relationships, we are really talking about *social capital*, or the networks between people—although, in terms of academic development, social capital can mean so much more. There is a direct and positive correlation between positive social capital and student achievement (Bourdieu, 1986; Coleman, 1988). Social capital and academic social networks support positive outcomes in education (Dika & Singh, 2002). Social capital—the right kind and the right amount—improves teaching, learning, and academic achievement (Mehan, 2012). Social capital can be a great equalizer in underrepresented populations, especially when students and families are taught effective networking techniques.

Students can benefit greatly from supportive institutional structures and family-school networks that invest in their lives and learning (Mussey, 2012). Moreover, simple social connections and interactions influence students' decision making and ability to persist in difficult fields, such as science, technology, engineering, and mathematics (Mussey, 2009). The literature in this field is rich and interesting and supports the use of cultivating connections as an approach for increasing SEL competencies.

It Starts With You

Cultivating connections starts with you. Remember when I told you that I didn't know my students' names. Well, here's the kicker: They didn't know mine either. Weird, huh? The truth is, during that first year of teaching, I barely knew my own name. I was so lost in the minutia of the daily grind that I had forgotten my purpose for being there in the first place. My to-do list had taken precedence over everything else in my life, including taking care of myself. If I wasn't taking care of myself, how could I possibly expect that I could care for 180 little people every single day?

Connecting With the Self

In some service industries, such as social work, there is an emphasis on self-care (Kinman & Grant, 2011). Sociologists and social workers often take entire courses on the topic. In fact, social workers have a core competency that addresses this idea (Newell & Nelson-Gardell, 2014), although I know some amazing social workers who would rather give everything that they own to others than take a moment for themselves.

I know many teachers who are in this self-sacrificing boat, too. I love these people. They are givers, and we need them on our planet. Unfortunately, among these wonderful humans, we are seeing stress, burnout, attrition, and worse (Schaefer et al., 2014). Emotional competency and self-care play a vital role in the resilience of professionals who serve others. If you are going to persist in the field of education—teaching, serving, and loving others day after day, year after year—you have to find ways to pause and connect with yourself. This type of self-care is vital and necessary for longevity and success in the field of education.

As an educator, take a moment to assess your current state regarding self-care with the Try This: Self-Care Assessment. For some of you, completing this checklist will be easy. Some of you are already doing many of these things, and it will be easy to say "yes, yes, yes." Good for you. Skip to the next section and start to use your amazing, centered self to connect with others and bring them up to the same level of self-care. For others of you, this assessment will be painful. It will be quick for you to say "no, no, no," and then you will realize that you need to start taking care of yourself, now. Good for you. Doing so will be a wonderful experience. For the rest of you, you are like me: Some of these things you are doing, and some you aren't—but you used to, and you want to, and you will again. Good for you—you are starting over. Let's get you back to caring for yourself emotionally and socially so that you can care for others, nurturing their social, emotional, and academic growth and development.

TRY THIS: Self-Care Assessment

Answer each of the following questions with a "yes" or "no." If you are unsure, you can decide whether to give yourself the benefit of the doubt or err on the side of caution. There is very little gray area in how I worded this list, but remember, this is a judgment-free zone.

Mindfulness in the Classroom

In the past week, have you:

	Yes	No
Engaged in exercise at least three times for at least 30 minutes?		
Gotten 6–8 hours of sleep each night?		
Prepared a healthy meal for yourself or asked someone else to do that for you?		
Planned to complete a short-term goal or action related to a longer term vision for your life?		
Laughed for a minute or more?		
Had an honest conversation with a friend, spouse, relative, or another human being who cares about you?		
Read something that made you think, feel, or act in a positive manner?		
Created a schedule for yourself that includes work and nonwork activities?		
Reflected and revised your schedule based on what really matters to you and your family?		
Realized that you made a mistake *and* forgiven yourself, or forgiven someone else for a mistake?		
Prayed, meditated, or written in a journal?		
Spent time doing something that you love that is not related to work?		
Spent time thinking about something really good that is happening in your life?		
Spent time resting that wasn't sleeping?		
Rewarded yourself or let someone reward you in some way for something that you accomplished?		

Cultivating Connections

My goal for everyone is that you will be able to answer "yes" to most of these questions most of the time, and all of these questions some of the time. Make sense? Let's see how you did.

If you answered "yes" to some of these questions, then you have been practicing positive self-care behaviors in one or more of the following areas: emotional health, relationships, physical well-being, spiritual growth, mental health, work-life balance.

If you answered "no" to most or every question, stop reading for a moment, take a deep breath, and close your eyes. Sit still and breathe with your eyes closed for a few minutes. Seriously, put this book down and do it. I'll wait . . .

There, now, isn't that better? Now, let's continue.

Like I said, the items on the checklist are positive behaviors related to self-care. When practiced habitually, they become our go-to coping mechanisms. Unfortunately, there are many negative behaviors that can replace these positive actions. Perhaps you have seen or participated in some of these as well. Negative coping mechanisms include things like:

- » drinking to the point of drunkenness,
- » taking illegal drugs,
- » smoking or using tobacco,
- » having angry outbursts or complaining excessively,
- » withdrawing from friends and family,
- » overeating/undereating,
- » working all of the time,
- » sleeping too much,
- » engaging in destructive relationships, and
- » engaging in excessive social media use or excess screen time.

This is not the time for guilt or shame. Most of us have used these or variations of some of these coping mechanisms during times of stress and to help us get through trials. You made it through. What matters now is that you become aware that there are healthy and unhealthy ways to cope. Choose healthy. Trials will come, guaranteed. Trials have a way of stretching us and helping us grow. Of course, in the midst of trouble, it is sometimes hard to find that positive perspective. Plan ahead by practicing healthy coping strategies that you can use when the storm clouds begin to form. Initiating positive coping mechanisms today can promote productivity, health, and success, even when the struggle gets real.

Positive self-care is something that you have to bring into your conscious awareness. It is an exercise in mindfulness that requires intentionality. Imagine combining all of the positive coping mechanisms that you have learned and developing an intentional self-care plan (see Figure 7). Social workers are taught to do this (University at Buffalo, 2018). Teachers can and should do this, too. Let's be more proactive about how we cope with the demanding work that we do. Our default reactions can often include reactive stress, poor time management, and carelessness, which can lead to mental, physical, spiritual, emotional, and/or relational issues. Creation of a self-care plan enables you to be proactive about your well-being. Social-emotional competence increases, and your mental, physical, relational, and career health will improve as a result. Positive coping leads to positive outcomes (Folkman & Moskowitz, 2000).

When you decide to invest some time into self-care, you will have more time to care for and serve others. The results will be an increased ability to cope, increased happiness, and more joy.

TRY THIS: Self-Care Plan

Using the following questions as a guide, develop a daily or weekly self-care plan:

1. What morning routine will help you prepare for what you want to accomplish? (Examples: Meditate, create a schedule, set a goal, exercise, eat a healthy breakfast, etc.)
2. How will you achieve a healthy work-life balance? (Examples: Plan a time to accomplish work tasks, plan a time to do something enjoyable that is not related to work, etc.)

Self-Care Plan	
Mind	Body
Spirit	Emotions

FIGURE 7. Self-care planning template.

3. How will you stimulate yourself mentally? What will you read, listen to, or watch that will help you grow in your knowledge of teaching and learning?
4. How will you maintain your physical health? (Examples: Make a healthy meal, take a 30-minute walk, etc.)
5. What negative behaviors would you like to replace?
6. How will you hold yourself accountable for creating this plan? (Examples: Create a calendar, get a buddy, use a journal, etc.)

Teach, Serve, Love

Now that you have spent some time connecting with yourself and reflecting on how you can care for your well-being in a regular, systematic way, let us turn our attention to others. Teaching is an act of service. It is an act of love. That understanding has become my motto and mantra for life: teach, serve, love. If you really want to teach, serve, and love others, you must connect with other people. You must learn to get along and play well with others. Teachers thrive when they are a part of a community of teachers, supporting and challenging one another to grow and improve for the sake of their students and the world.

So, how can you connect with others mindfully as you attempt to practice the art and science of teaching and learning? Teachers interact with so many people. How can we know how to do it well? Like many principles in this book, connecting with others can be easy when we apply some simple strategies to our interactions. When being mindful about connecting, I believe that there are some foundations and essentials that will radically improve your working relationships, regardless of whether you are thinking about working with students, staff, administrators, or parents. Let's discuss these ideas first, and then I'll provide a few activities that allow you to consider how these concepts might be differentiated to better serve the stakeholders that you may encounter. As you try the activities in the remainder of this chapter, consider connecting with others by posting what you are doing on social media with the hashtag #teachservelove.

Foundations: Eye Contact and Names

Think about the last time that you were having a heart-to-heart with your BFF. Did you look into that person's eyes? It's rather difficult if you are talking via text or social media, but if you are face-to-face, making the effort to make eye contact will go far to convey your sincerity and interest. Eye contact also allows you to understand the emotion behind the words that are said in the conversation. Making eye contact is important when we think about connecting with others. Remember that terrible classroom management story that I told you at the beginning of this chapter? Well, for me, making eye contact made all of the difference. That was my first step to knowing my students. I had to look at them and learn who they were. Making eye contact helped me to see them, their needs, and their unique strengths so that I could help them develop. Making eye contact also helped me see them so that I could learn their names. That was step two.

Confession: I am terrible at learning names. I have always struggled with it. As an introvert, sometimes all of my energy is used to think of what I am going to say next. When painful introductions are being made, I am usually so nervous about saying my name that I don't even hear what the other person says . . . unless I am being mindful about learning and remembering names. Using specific tricks and strategies is good place to start.

TRY THIS: Word Association

She says: "Hi, my name is Carolyn."

I think: Cooking Carolyn. I met her in my Cooking class. She likes Cookies.

Cookie Cooking Carolyn. Boom. I will never forget Carolyn. Using a mnemonic device or word association is extremely helpful in remembering names.

You can use this activity as an icebreaker with students. In that case, allow students to choose their own word associations, and go around the room having students identify others using mnemonics. Within the first day of class, everyone will be familiar with each other's names, an important factor for building community and unity.

Of course, the ultimate learn-their-names strategy is to make a seating chart. Memorize the seating chart. You might also take students' pictures and create a community board or wall of fame. Get to know students by identifying something you like about each of them.

Making eye contact and learning names build the foundation for connecting with students. Build a solid foundation, and relationships will grow from there. Here are the essentials for building true connections with other humans (see Figure 8).

Essential #1: Be Humble

Remember this: You are not too busy or too important. Teaching is about relationships and service. In order to effectively serve others, you must gladly lower yourself before them with humility. You must refuse to be too busy to make time for people. You must willingly stop, listen, and learn from others, especially from those who are lower than you on the chain of command, including your students. You must become less than and make them greater. You must willingly raise them up.

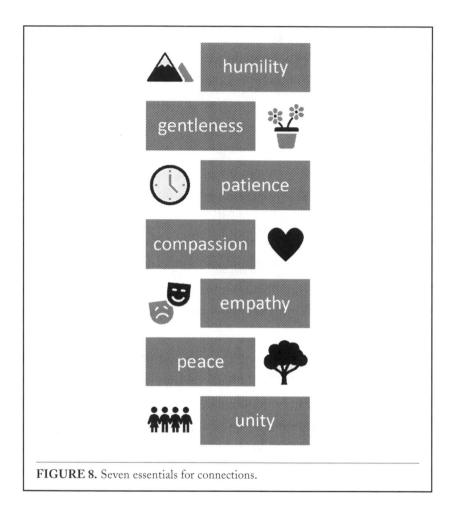

FIGURE 8. Seven essentials for connections.

Humility is defined as a low opinion of one's importance. This essential is hard for me. In fact, it almost drove me out of education for good. Humility is a wonderful thing and absolutely critical for growth. I'm glad I learned this before it was too late. But, honestly, I had to learn the hard way. My pride was rampant, and I didn't even know it. I had to experience loneliness and failure before I figured out that I wasn't too busy or important to work with and for others. There are still days when I struggle with humility, and I am always thankful when I am reminded that I don't always have the answers. I am still

Cultivating Connections

learning and growing along with everyone else. I will be a learner forever, and for that I am truly humbled (and grateful).

The opposite of humility is pride, which can manifest in many ways (see Figure 9), most of them detrimental to our ability to serve others well. One of the ways that pride shows up in our lives is in perfectionism. Perfectionists are not keen on making mistakes. But it is impossible to become a master educator without making and learning from your mistakes. This is an essential part of the development process. It is impossible to grow in the classroom if you are not willing to risk failure.

Pride can also be expressed by finding fault in everyone but yourself. This characteristic will not work in the classroom. If all of your students are struggling, there is only one person to blame: you. Humble yourself. Search yourself and see how you can work harder and what you can do to help your students learn. Ask for help and help others. Sometimes it *is* your fault, but if you stay humble and learn, everything will be OK.

How can one develop humility? There are several habits of the humble that you can practice when connecting with teachers, parents, and students. Consider the following ideas:

» Find something positive that each student brings to the classroom community. Make a list of these positive attributes and spend some time thinking about and appreciating your students' strengths. Notice how your students are different than you and sometimes more skilled than you in some areas. What can you learn from them? Make a list.

» Seek out the help of other teachers who know more than you. Also, seek out the help of other teachers who know less than you. Listen to their guidance and try some of their ideas. Write them thank-you notes.

» Ask your principal why he or she chose to be a principal. Do not make assumptions. Consider how his or her leadership contributes to the success of the campus.

» Put the needs of others first. Consider how you might be able to help the families of your students before you ask them to

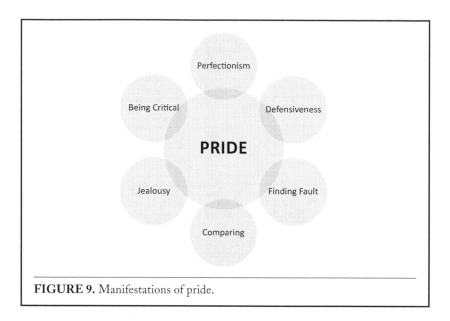

FIGURE 9. Manifestations of pride.

help you. Reach out to them in a "Reverse-Volunteer" news-letter. Instead of soliciting their help for classroom activities, offer your assistance in their lives. Do not assume that you know what they need. Ask them, and then follow through with your service.

» Congratulate another teacher for his or her accomplishments (especially if you find yourself feeling jealous or resentful). This is huge. There are plenty of opportunities to succeed. Someone else's success does not mean your failure. Start operating from an attitude of accepting abundance.

» Ask a colleague for feedback on a lesson plan and make changes as they are suggested. Share your success with your colleague and practice gratitude by writing that person a thank-you note or giving a small gift. Appreciate how others can help you improve.

Cultivating Connections

Teach Students to Be Humble

Much of the previous list is transferable to students. For example, you might ask your students to create a list that names something positive about each of their classmates. In this way, they can celebrate the gifts that each student contributes to the classroom community. Is it feasible for your students to interview you and ask you why you are a teacher? Help them understand your methods and motivations for teaching them. The interview may provide you with an opportunity to explicitly tell students that you care about their academic, social, and emotional learning and well-being and that you are investing in their future. Tell them about a teacher who invested in your future in a similar way. Practice humility as your students ask you questions. When you model this behavior, students will follow your lead. Be the humble yet effective leader that they need.

TRY THIS: Put Others' Needs First

Read the following story, which has been adapted from Dave Ramsey (2018). Then answer the questions that follow.

> Once upon a time, a group of soldiers was traveling through a heavily wooded area. When the soldiers came up to a particularly narrow part of the road, they realized that their convoy couldn't continue without moving a heavy log that blocked the west side of the road.
>
> As the corporal on horseback watched, the foot soldiers struggled to move the log. The log wouldn't budge. They needed a hand. A rider approached. He observed the situation and called out to the corporal, "Sir, why are you not helping these men?" The corporal answered, "I am the corporal, sir. I give the orders."
>
> The rider silently dismounted. He walked through the mud and over to the log. He took hold, and together the rider and the foot soldiers successfully moved the log. The soldiers and

the rider parted ways, but not without a quick salute and a smile. Who was this kind rider, you ask? It was George Washington, the commander-in-chief.

1. Compare the behavior of the corporal and the commander-in-chief.
2. Reflect on ways the commander put others' needs first. How did he exhibit humility in his actions? What was the result?
3. Whom do you identify with in the story?

No Preferential Treatment

Another way that you can teach humility is by honoring and encouraging your students *without favoritism*. Favoritism provokes pride and tips the balance of equity, disadvantaging some while growing others' unearned sense of entitlement. If you hold equity as a core value, it is essential to abolish preferential treatment from your classroom.

Unfortunately, we are not always aware when we use preferential treatment. We must be mindful and intentional about how we teach without bias. One simple way to begin to address favoritism is by randomly selecting students for certain tasks. Write their names on popsicle sticks and draw a name. Make sure everyone gets selected at some point in the lesson. This is a classic yet effective maneuver that will reduce bias in how and whom you engage.

You may not know that you operate with subconscious bias. Some of our preferences, deeply embedded within our consciousness, are hidden, even from ourselves. To learn about your own biases, you might consider asking for feedback. Be careful how and whom you ask. As you attempt to expose and address your biases, you might experience shame, hurt, or even guilt. Continue the process. As you become more self-aware, you will be better able to regulate your behavior. As you become mindful about issues of equity, your practices will reflect your desired values. You will be able to create a culture of equity in your sphere of influence, leading by example. Do the work. It will be worth it.

Essential #2: Be Gentle

When I was a little girl, my mom painted a sign to hang in our living room. It was orange with white letters carefully stenciled in the center: *Moderation*. That sign comes to mind often as I rush around, trying to get my long, self-created to-do list done. Occasionally, I will find myself hurrying about in a near rage. My words and actions are angry and harsh; there is too much on my plate, and I feel wild and out of control.

Generally, when I get into this harried state, I realize that I have forgotten that wise word from my mom. I realize that I'm doing too much. Sometimes when I get into this zone of overcommitment and stress, I will call my mom. With a simple word or two, her gentle and generous spirit can help me calm down and prioritize what matters in this life. Her gentleness, supported by her mantra of moderation, can make all of the difference.

Gentleness is a quality characterized by kindness and tenderness. When I say the word *gentle*, who comes to mind for you? Think about how this person interacts with the world. People who are gentle have a manner that is mild and careful. Gentleness is a strength. The power that a gentle word or action can have is mesmerizing.

I believe that there is a misconception among preservice teachers that effective classroom management requires dominance and harshness. This simply isn't so. Some of the most effective educators that I have known possess a gentle spirit that is simply captivating to their students and colleagues alike. Consider how it feels to be around them.

Gentle people reduce stress. Their mere presence may lower the negative emotions that students are coping with when they are learning a difficult concept or interacting with a difficult peer. Gentle people bring calmness to any situation. They are not reactive and are often seen as pillars of the community. Gentleness is not weakness—quite the contrary. In order to be gentle, you must possess a confidence in your capabilities and a patience in dealing with others.

How Can You Practice Being Gentler?

One of the greatest tools that I utilize to grow in this way is to surround myself with gentle humans. I attempt to emulate their actions, their ways of speaking and doing things. I listen to what they say and, most importantly, how they say it.

Another effective tool for becoming gentle is silence. There are times when silence, contemplation, and waiting are necessary. Practicing silence can help you avoid a negative, knee-jerk reaction. Be still and wait.

Essential #3: Be Patient

Not everything is an emergency. Not everything needs an instant answer or an instantly gratifying response. *Be patient.*

My dad is a master craftsman. His preferred medium is wood. With expert carpentry skills, he can build anything with little to no margin of error. His tricks: precision and patience. Measure twice, cut once, and be patient. Craftsmanship requires patience. Sometimes, when it rains, you wait for the rain to stop. There are woodworking materials that won't dry in the rain. My dad has patience. Patience is an essential principle to developing positive connections with students in schools.

Be Patient With People

I think the actual term here is *grace*. Grace in movement is evident by a refinement or elegance exhibited in action. In relationships, grace is an unearned, undeserved benefit, service, or blessing bestowed upon another. Consider when you might have experienced grace or received an undeserved favor or forgiveness from another person. Perhaps you wronged someone, and he or she never mentioned it. Perhaps a debt was excused. Perhaps a humiliation was avoided at another's expense.

Grace allows us to be patient, waiting until the time is right, not for us, but for others. It is a gift that is freely given and greatly appreciated.

Be Patient With Learning

Learning is a process. It takes time, and it happens differently for every individual. Do what you are supposed to be doing to facilitate learning, and then wait. Apply the research-based practices that are proven to be effective, and then let them work (Bransford et al., 2000). It takes time. If you struggle with impatience in this area, there are a couple of tools that will support you as you wait.

As students work, make observations. Measure their progress incrementally. As learning progresses, track achievement using data. Enjoy observing the learning without intervening for a moment. Chart data in a visual format that will show you that even though you are waiting, there is something happening. This is a lesser-known use for data: developing patience.

While students work, do some research and determine extension ideas for your lessons. That way, once students know what you need them to know, you can all move forward together. Research fills idle time, and while students' brains are busy, yours can be, too. Be patient with learning. Teach students to be patient, too. Learning is rarely about the product, and the process requires patience.

Essential #4: Practice Empathy

Try to see the world through the eyes of a stranger, and you will start to see the power of *empathy*, the ability to feel the way someone else feels without actually having to go through their experiences. Empathy can change the world. Imagine if school shooters could think about and feel what grieving parents, siblings, and friends of victims feel. Imagine if these feelings could influence decisions. The truth is, they can. When we feel for others, we can react in ways that support their needs. We will comfort the sad, celebrate with the cheerful, and eliminate hurting one another in such blatant and preventable ways. This kind of empathy is needed.

How can we promote empathy? One way that I have seen empathy developed in short amounts of time is through candid and critical conversations (Patterson, 2012). In order for these conversations to occur, a safe space must be created. Prompts and facilitation can help promote these types of conversations.

TRY THIS: Conversation Blooms

Develop 3–5 provocative questions designed to promote empathy. Some examples of empathy-provoking questions include:

- What should people better understand about you?
- What is a dream that you have had for a long time, and why haven't you accomplished it yet? What do you wish the world knew about your dream?
- Who has helped you become better than you once were? What did they do?
- What is an obstacle that you have overcome, and how did you overcome it? What do you want people to understand about that experience?

Select one question to be examined by a group of colleagues. This works well with a group of educators who are supporting the same students and must work together to ensure the success of their students. This activity allows the teachers to talk about themselves and the things they are passionate about. It also gives teachers insight into how much they want others to understand them and how this understanding affects how they operate in the workplace. Through these conversations, teachers can see similarities between themselves and others. Shared experiences and shared struggles become fertile grounds for future empathetic interactions. Consider sharing your experience with these conversations on social media using the hashtag #teachservelove. I'd love to connect with you and learn from you.

Essential #5: Practice Compassion

I once heard compassion described as "love in action" (V. Stone, personal correspondence, n.d.). *Webster's Dictionary* defines compassion as "the intense desire to help someone in need; a sympathetic consciousness of another's distress and a desire to alleviate it."

As a teacher, I have seen, felt, and a responded to humans in distress. Students feel distress when they are not learning or achieving at school. Students feel distress because of other, real-life circumstances that are beyond their control (e.g., homelessness, hunger, abuse). Parents feel distress because of a loss or lack of understanding about what to do with distressed children. Teachers feel distress when their dream of making a difference in the world is confronted by the reality of a bureaucratic school system. Teachers feel distress when they encounter real and perceived barriers to teaching that are embedded in the sociological institution that we call school. Distress is real, y'all. As teachers, we must respond in compassionate and effective ways.

Compassion in Action

I don't know about you, but I don't recall taking any courses on compassionate responses to academic or other distress calls. Did you? If so, bravo! Please refer more people to your preparatory program. Most of us did not. Unlike in social work, compassion is not an explicit value in education. Although many educators practice compassion and hold this value dear in their own lives and behaviors, this quality is not universally practiced across the classrooms in American schools. Why not? Could we do a better job at helping individuals grow in this area? Absolutely.

We need educators to be compassionate. How are we to respond to distress in our students and ourselves if we lack the skills or strategies necessary to do so in a compassionate way? Model compassionate responses in your daily interactions. For example, when a colleague approaches you with a complaint about a student, respond first by saying, "I understand." Then, instead of contributing to the negative commentary, ignoring the issue, or walking away, ask, "How can I help you teach your student?" Take the time to follow through with helping and follow up with your colleague by asking, "How is your student doing now? How are you feeling now?"

When a student is underperforming uncharacteristically, respond with compassion. Seek to understand why the student is not meeting your expectations. Set aside a time to meet with the student and talk. With genuine care, ask the student what happened. Wait for his or her response. Offer to help the student. Follow through and follow up.

TRY THIS: Compassion Contracts

Work with your class to create a list of 3–5 ways that your students will care for each other and the community. Create this "compassion contract" together and have students sign the contract. In the days and weeks that follow, hold each other accountable for fulfilling your compassionate goals. An example of a "compassion contract" is below.

We, the undersigned, agree to act with compassion in our classroom. We will demonstrate compassion in the following ways:
1. We will help our friends problem solve when we see them struggling in math. We will never laugh at their mistakes when they are trying.
2. We will smile and sit next to friends who seem lonely.
3. We will use our hands to hug and give high fives to our friends who need encouragement.

Signed,
Dr. Mussey's Class

TRY THIS: Class Pet or Class Garden

OK, I know this is a cliché. But class pets and/or plants can teach kids how to care for living things. Make explicit how the behaviors/characteristics of caring for the animal or plant can be transferred to caring for humans. Take pictures of your class pets and gardens and share them with your community or post them on social media with the hashtag #teachservelove.

Just feeling for other people isn't enough. As Mr. Rogers said, "It is what we do with these feelings that matter" (Neville, Ma, & Capotosto, 2018). Compassion practices teach students to act on their feelings in ways that improve the lives of others.

Essential #6: Be Peaceful

When practicing Principle 3: Cultivating Connections, you will often realize that context is very important. Learning essentials, such as humility, gentleness, patience, empathy, and compassion, require a safe place. In order to use these practices to develop social and emotional competencies in teachers and students, you must create this safe place in your classroom. SEL requires a *place of peace*. Think of your peaceful classroom space as the incubator for positive growth. As you and your students grow in the areas of humility, patience, grace, empathy, and compassion, your space will become even more peaceful as you become peaceful. Once initiated, this is an iterative, self-sustaining process. Try to be intentional about creating a place of peace this year.

Peace Out

In order to create a place of peace, first consider the physical space. Are there ways that you can utilize the senses to promote peace? For example, consider what peace looks like. Can you paint the wall or bring in a carpet or poster with a calm, peaceful atmosphere? Blues and greens are colors of peace. What does peace sound like? Can you limit chaotic auditory input and create moments of silence? Can you play peaceful music? What does peace smell like? Can you tap into what we know about the brain and use natural, peace-invoking scents in your classroom (e.g., lavender or jasmine)?

If it is not possible to manipulate your physical space, can you create an inner peaceful space by allowing a time for students to close their eyes and breathe deeply and calmly? When you do this, a naturally produced hormone called *oxytocin* is released, stimulating calmness and relaxing the mind and other physical organs. This is an excellent example of teaching with the brain in mind (Jensen, 2005). Try it. Breathe deep. Peace is essential.

Essential #7: Promote Unity

When attempting to help others build connections, it is essential to promote unity. What is the common goal? What is the common vision? As a teacher and leader, your job is to create and communicate this concept to your classroom community. Be empowered to operate as a community with a shared journey, because that is what you are. Have you been in classes with no sense of purpose? How much more did you learn when you were striving together toward some common goal? For many years, I've had a banner in my classroom that says, "Better together." Yes, we are better together. Believe that and teach that to your students.

Connections and SEL

When you are engaged in mindfully pursuing connections with others in your school community, you are developing social and emo-

Cultivating Connections

tional competencies. Consider the self-awareness that you learn as you intentionally become more humble, gentle, and patient. Self-regulation occurs with initiating humility and patience, too. In order to be empathetic, you have to be socially aware. Responding to the needs of others in an empathetic way builds relationships. Social awareness is also developed as you strive to dismiss favoritism and promote equity. Finally, when you are uniting people, as a team of peaceful learners, you will make responsible decisions that build relationships, too. Connecting with yourself, students, and staff requires and develops SEL while simultaneously making the world a more peaceful and joyful place to exist.

Love Over Tolerance

Ultimately, cultivating connections is about infusing more love into your teaching and learning. It is about loving yourself, your students, and your environment. This mindfulness approach dwarfs the minimum standard of tolerance. Tolerance isn't enough. In order to truly connect with each other, we need to love one another. Love is the key to all of the essentials. It is the umbrella under which all of the other essentials fall. Can you be gentle or compassionate without loving people? No. Can you be patient and graceful, forgiving the mistakes of others without love? Impossible.

TRY THIS: Love Columns

On a sheet of paper, create a chart with three columns. In the first column, write down the name of every one of your students. In the next column, write one thing that you love about each person. Try to think of things that go beyond the surface level of appreciation. In the final column, commit to one thing that you will do this year to show each individual the love that you have for him or her. Do the things. An example of a love columns chart is on the next page.

Person's Name	What I Love About This Person	How I Can Demonstrate This Love
Brian	I love how Brian is calm in all situations.	I can demonstrate love to Brian by writing him a personal note thanking him for his presence and composure.
Max	I love how Max designs monster truck race tracks using raw materials creatively and expertly.	I can demonstrate love to Max by sitting with him as he builds and asking him questions that spark his joy and imagination.
Sarah	I love how Sarah selflessly cares for her students in class.	I can demonstrate love to Sarah by bringing her a cup of coffee in the morning.
Richard	I love how Richard has devoted his life to teaching students with special needs and coaching students in wrestling.	I can demonstrate love to Richard by attending one of his coaching events and cheering for his kids.

This activity can also be useful for getting to know and appreciate your fellow teachers. Complete the same activity, but place teachers' names in the left column. If you don't know them, go meet them. Learn about them and learn from them.

In Summary

We, as teachers, must bring back the love to our work. We must not merely tolerate, but love, every single one of our students, colleagues, and ourselves. Teachers need other teachers, and we must learn how to better love and serve one another so that we may better

Cultivating Connections

love and serve our students. This is our highest calling and at the core of what we must do each and every day.

Discussion Questions

1. Discuss the importance of creating a self-care plan. Reflect on the status of your personal self-care plan. What are three positive coping mechanisms that you would like to try this school year? Why?

2. List the essentials in cultivating connections. Which of the seven essentials do you find the most challenging in your teaching practice? Who on your campus is particularly good at this essential? How might you humble yourself and ask for help in this area?

3. Social workers sometimes experience a phenomenon called *compassion fatigue*, a condition in which compassion decreases over time due to the frequency of appeals to meet the needs of those suffering. Do you think that teachers could experience compassion fatigue also? If so, what coping mechanisms might be utilized to address this issue?

4. Discuss the idea of love in schools. On a scale of 1–10, how is your campus doing in the area of loving and demonstrating love to students? Discuss three strategies for improving this practice. Why is love more important than tolerance?

Journal Prompt

When you think about your upcoming school year, how do you want your students to interact with one another and with you? What is your role in promoting this kind of interaction? Commit to trying one activity that you read about in this chapter. Return to this journal entry to reflect on what happened as a result of your efforts.

Writing

We are all apprentices in a craft where no one ever becomes a master.

—Ernest Hemingway

The relationship between thought and word is a living process: thought is born of words; A word devoid of thought is a dead thing, and a thought without a word remains a shadow.

—Lev Vygotsky

Training Day

When I was 28, I set a goal to run a marathon before I turned 30. There were only a few problems with this goal: (1) I didn't like to run and (2) I didn't run. Hmmm . . . I signed up anyway. I remember the first running practice with my new team. I didn't even own a pair of running shoes, and my cotton t-shirt and shorts were clear indications that I was the rookie.

 DOI: 10.4324/9781003236665-9

Mindfulness in the Classroom

Talk about intimidation. I walked up to find a group of athletes wearing the newest, technologically sound, moisture-wicking running gear, noticeably fit with toned legs and worn-in, professionally fitted sneakers. As I looked down at my cross trainers and pasty, flabby thighs, I considered turning around and heading back to the car.

But then someone tapped my shoulder. With a genuine smile and a gentle spirit, my new friend Vera welcomed me. She assured me that she would run with me that day.

She did. Step-by-step, she stayed next to me as I finished a grueling, 2-mile trek down a flat road on a perfect and sunny San Diego morning.

I ran! I actually ran! I felt like an Olympian that morning. It was really hard, but I did it. And, the next Saturday morning, I did it again—3 miles this time. The next week, I ran 4 miles. Each week, I increased my mileage and confidence incrementally. Of course, in marathon training, there are also down weeks and tapering sessions when you do less. These are moments when you can check in with yourself, giving your legs and lungs time to heal and rebuild. Then, you add more.

In October 2006, I completed my first marathon. Over the next several years, I would log thousands of miles on these flabby thighs. They wouldn't always be flabby, and the warm San Diego sunshine would erase the paste. I would find my own moisture-wicking attire and buy dozens of my own fancy and professionally fitted running shoes.

I love running. It is my go-to exercise. Even when my knee is creaking and popping, as it does now, I can find freedom and flow when I am pounding the pavement. But remember how I started. I wasn't running, and I didn't like to run. I have found few things in life that compared to this experience until now. Writing, like running, starts at the beginning.

Writing

Discipline

When I started writing, I didn't like to write, and I didn't write. I was 20 and trying to finish my biology degree at Texas A&M University. My cell biology professor asked us to write a paper. The nerve! Scientists didn't write, or so I thought.

I had to start somewhere, and just like that first running practice, I showed up to the first day. I sat down at the computer, and painstakingly typed out a sentence, the equivalent of that first 2-mile run. Ouch. It hurt, but I did it.

Each day, I found my way back to the keys and wrote more. Writing, like running, is a discipline, requiring daily attention, mental preparation, the proper materials, and a designated time allotment. In running, discipline requires attention to a daily nutrition plan and stretching beforehand, mental toughness and hydration during, and foam rolling afterward. Similarly, writing requires research and pre-writing beforehand, mental toughness and persistence during, and reflection and editing afterward. And, just like running, believe it or not, writing does not have to be a solitary pursuit. Today I love to run and write.

Benefits

For me, writing is a way to intentionally process my thoughts and formulate them into coherent ideas. I like the process of ideas becoming words. Those words form sentences, paragraphs, and even books sometimes. Writing has many other benefits as well:

- » Writing is metacognitive; it increases your consciousness about the world around you.
- » Writing is mindful and can promote SEL in yourself and your students (Hooker & Fodor, 2008; Medrano, 2017).
- » Writing is an art—a creative process that can be taught, practiced, nurtured, and developed.

» Writing is a technical skill that can be taught. There are formulas and rules for writing. But more importantly, writing is a process that requires writers to write, revise, and repeat (Becker, 2007).
» There is freedom in the creative expression of writing.
» Writing is a way to process thoughts, feelings, and emotions.
» Writing is a pathway toward intellectual pursuits.
» Writing is essential to communication and the future (National Writing Project, 2011).

A Social Tool

Language is a social tool, and writing is a wonderful expression of produced language. Lev Vygotsky (1978) laid the foundation for our understanding of learning as a social endeavor, advocating for the learner to be surrounded by language and opportunities to communicate. He noted the motivating effects of social interaction. Consider how motivated your students might be if allowed to use writing as a social tool, knowing that it will be authentic and purposeful. Vygotsky also taught us that social interaction and communication lead to higher mental functioning. There is a connection between external language and internal thought, and writing is often the link. He called the process of using inner speech to formulate external communication the "thought-language cycle." This cycle enables us to plan, regulate, and produce concepts and ideas. Writing is thinking (Zinsser, 1990). Writing effectively requires the critical thinking skills of analysis, synthesis, and evaluation.

The research on writing tells us that this thought-language cycle is recursive; it is necessary during each phase of the writing process, especially the prewriting and composition phases (Everson, 1991). This idea of internal processing has been further developed and studied by cognitive scientists and neuroscientists. When processing, students make and clarify meaning by thinking and then communicating

Writing

a thought through spoken or written language. It is a continuous process that results in learning. Writing is learning.

Because writing is vital for learning, why not let students write as often as possible, using new technology and tools in creative ways? Consider the positive aspects of using digital media in your writing instruction. It is a quick and effective mode of communication, provides easy access to resources, allows collaboration, and can provide a source of constant and immediate encouragement. Of course, teachers, parents, and communities must first address some of the negative aspects of social media, like bullying (Lenhart, Madden, Smith, Purcell, & Zickuhr, 2011). However, once safety is ensured, there may be a great benefit to using social media to teach and learn writing, including the chance to share student writing with an authentic audience (Heitin, 2011), a wonderful and necessary experience for writers of every level.

All Roads Lead to Writing

Given the cognitive, social, and motivational benefits, it is easy to conclude that writing is a wonderful tool for teachers and students. Beyond these benefits, writing can also be used to promote mindfulness and SEL in the classroom (Mani, 2014). Writing can be mindful, both in form and function. For example, given the nature of narrative writing, self-awareness is often an implicit result. Similarly, the process of journal writing raises the consciousness of the writer, allowing him or her the time to intentionally focus on a well-developed prompt or question. In both narrative writing and journaling, the process and product can be part of a mindful exploration of self that helps people know who they are and what they believe.

Beyond the personal and academic benefits, writing is a necessary skill in many career fields. People are expected to communicate in writing in almost any work environment. This wasn't always the case, but technology has increased our need to clearly communicate with the written word. Moreover, writing is often used in business to introduce, invite, persuade, negotiate, and resolve conflicts. Successful people know how to write well. As teachers, if we are truly invested in seeing our students succeed in life, we must teach them how to write, regardless of what subject or grade-level we teach.

If all teachers are writing teachers, we need to think of ourselves in this way. We need to be trained in writing instructional methods and learn to teach writing well. We must teach the writing process to our students one step at a time. As they move from one phase to the next, their skills will grow, and eventually they will be writing on their own.

The mindfulness principle of writing calls for change. This change requires a shift in the mindset of teachers to believe that we all can and should teach writing. When enough teachers change their mindsets and behaviors, campus cultures begin to change, too. Often, this change begins in the walls of the classroom with the teacher at the forefront.

Like writing, change takes time and practice. And, like running, sometimes you need someone with you on the path. You are better able to move through the process with a more capable individual as a guide. So, how can you guide your students to write more effectively and to use writing to learn? How can you become the more capable guide? You must write, too.

A Writing Habit

Establish a "writing place" for yourself. This could be a corner of your home or classroom. Make this place special and comfortable. My writing place is a creaky chair pulled up to my farmhouse kitchen table. I open the window shade so that I can see the oak trees in my backyard. I clear everything else off of the table and place a soft yellow pillow behind my back. Before I get settled in, I make myself a hot cup of coffee. I make sure that my computer is charged and that I have three inspirational texts at arm's reach. I start by finding a quote or photograph that is related to my topic of the day. As I retype the quote, my writing session begins.

Writing

When I am writing, I typically set a page goal for the day. I try to remain in my creaky chair until that goal is met. This is my writing ritual. This is how I have trained myself to get started. Without this habit, I wouldn't get anything done.

Once I have some words on the page, the real work begins. As in a marathon, sometimes the last milestones are the hardest to cross. Initial drafts morph into edited pages and rewrites. Page goals become revision schedules, and pages upon pages are added, deleted, and added again. Writing is a process, and it requires daily discipline and time.

TRY THIS: The 21-Day Writing Challenge

Establish a writing place for yourself. Once you have a place, establish a habit. For the next 21 days, spend some time in your writing place. Assign yourself a writing task and a page goal for each day, and then get to work. If possible, write at the same time every day. Keep that time sacred and don't cancel on yourself. Your writing task could be a simple journal reflection. It could involve anecdotal notes about your day. It could be a stream-of-consciousness writing experiment in which you write everything that comes to mind. Just start writing and see what happens. If you are going to lead your students to write more effectively, create a writing habit for yourself first. If you can do it for yourself, then you can do the same for them.

TRY THIS: Writing Prompts for Mindfulness

Give your students the 21-day writing challenge. Give them time to write and set the expectation for that time. Writing time is sacred. How will you communicate that? Develop writing prompts that are important and relevant to your students. Consider issues going on in America today. Allow students to become aware of themselves and the world through their writing habit. Here are 21 writing prompts for mindfulness to get you started:

1. What does the world need more of now?
2. What are you most afraid of doing?
3. Does technology unite or divide us?
4. Think about the last time you experienced joy. Write about it.
5. What are the qualities that you want most in a friend?
6. What are the qualities that you want most in a teacher? Write a job advertisement for this person.
7. Write a guide for getting along with others.
8. If you could change the world, what would you do? Why? How?
9. Who is someone who has helped you in your life? Write that person a thank-you note.
10. Should manufacturers make boys' shoes available in pink?
11. Is it hard being a girl?
12. What do you do when you are having a bad day?
13. What makes you sad? How do you handle this emotion?
14. What are three things that make you proud?
15. Who is one person you trust? Describe that person.
16. If you could change one thing about America, what would you change? Why?
17. If you could spend a week on a remote island, what three items would you bring? Why?
18. What is one word that describes your current mood? Why?
19. What happened to you today? Write your story.
20. If you had your own talk show, who would you want to interview? What questions would you ask?
21. Today, I am grateful for . . .

Writing, Mindfulness, and SEL

How might a writing prompt allow you to support students in their social and emotional development? Let us look at the following writing prompt: *Write a guide for getting along with others.*

Writing

Consider how you might use this prompt to talk about relationship skills, social awareness, and responsible decision making. As students reflect on themselves and the ways that they get along with others, they become more self-aware. As they think about how getting along requires empathy, compromise, and communication, they become socially aware. Finally, writing a guide requires students to think about the decisions that need to be made in order to build relationships and get along with others. This writing prompt is a wonderful starting point for supporting the development of self-awareness, social awareness, relationship skills, and responsible decision making. Consider how you might take a simple prompt and create a lesson or unit for SEL.

TRY THIS: Think-Write-Share

Think about something you have a great deal of experience doing (e.g., teaching, parenting, swimming, cooking, drawing, walking). Now, take a walk down memory lane to a time when you were less experienced in this area. Can you remember how you felt as a beginner? Can you remember the first time you tried this activity? Were you instantly good? Who helped you? How did you improve? What supplies were needed? How did you grow and develop the skills needed to persist? How do you feel about the activity now?

Reflect on the answers to those questions in writing. Now, create a timeline of your experience, highlighting several important milestones. Share how you can apply this learning process to your teaching, especially as you learn to teach writing.

In the beginning, writing is hard; this is the nature of being a novice. But as you move from novice to expert in any subject area, you will improve, and so will your students. In order to embrace writing as a learning and thinking tool, you need to build efficacy in yourself and your students. As you do, you will become more proficient. If you are going to use writing as a principle of mindfulness and a way to develop SEL, there are three essentials.

Essential #1: All Teachers Are Writing Teachers

When I was teaching seventh-grade science, my department required every student to conduct his or her own science fair project. It was amazing—truly, a science teacher's dream. I loved the idea of my students being able to select a problem and investigate it using the scientific method. I planned and plotted with my fellow teachers. I invited community members and friends to the science fair. I had high expectations that it would be grand. After all, we had taught our students science, and it was their time to shine.

We set the due date and distributed the formatting requirements and grading rubrics. We told students to start early. Upon completion of their experiment, they would create a trifold display board and a science notebook, including a seven-part research paper with references. We wished them luck.

The due date arrived. I couldn't be more excited to see the innovative ideas on display. The students arrived, display board in one hand, notebook in the other. We started the judging process with anticipation.

I picked up the first paper that I was supposed to evaluate and started to read. It only took two sentences for my hopes to be dashed. I moved on to the next project. This time, I started with the display board. When an incomplete sentence greeted me, I lowered my head. As I moved through the room, reading students' papers and trying to make sense of their displays, disappointment and shame flooded my heart. I could feel my face flush as I looked around the room at the work that the kids had made. As proud as I was of their efforts and some of the science that they attempted to communicate, we had a problem: the writing.

Writing

The good news is that when you give a group of science teachers a problem, they immediately set out to solve it—and that is what we did. We hypothesized, gathered evidence, and began to draw some conclusions.

We looked at many variables: different English teachers, different experiments, different printer ink. What could it be? We needed to find the one thing that all of the students had in common—the common denominator, the culprit, the consistent and unchanging variable that could not be denied by the scientific mind. Gasp! It was us! We were their teachers, and, when we analyzed the data, we could only draw one viable conclusion: Our students did not know how to write (in science class) because we had not taught them.

I realized something wonderful and terrifying at the same time. That day, I temporarily took off my science teacher hat and set it to the side. I stood up tall and said these words aloud: "I am a writing teacher. I will teach them to write."

When the entire science department decided that we would use scaffolds and processes, as well as templates and timelines, to teach our students how to write their science papers, we saw the powerful effects. In just one short year of being mindful about how to teach writing in science, we saw improvements. We wore three hats that year as scientist-teacher-writers. The results surprised us. Not only did our students' writing improve, but their science improved, too. We were using writing as a strategy to teach science. We were mindful about how we scaffolded the process. We learned that when we teach students, they learn. Our students became good science writers. We began to believe that, with the right supports, our students could do just about anything.

Writing Across the Curriculum

Part of this mindful work is changing mindsets. This requires a shift in thinking for teachers who don't believe that they can or should be teaching writing. We are all writing teachers. Writing involves thinking, reflection, and processing, as well as communicating. It can be utilized across all ages and across all curriculum areas. This is not a new idea, but it is one that we need to revisit.

Writing across the curriculum (WAC) is a movement to support the idea that we are all writing teachers, and that all students need to learn to write in all content areas. The WAC movement gained ground in the 1970s, and since then it has been implemented in campuses at all levels. Like any idea or movement in our field, momentum for WAC has ebbed and flowed like the tide. Also, like any popular concept or phrase in our field, definitions and original intentions have been muddied over time.

In 1987, McLeod and others tried to bring some clarification to the ways in which universities were implementing WAC programs and practice. In conclusion, McLeod said that WAC is really about change—programmatic, curricular, and behavioral change. In addition, WAC is about change in learning processes. Writing engages learners in more active processing, transforming learning environments into literacy-rich places of thinking and communicating. If a campus culture has embraced WAC, social learning and the thought-language cycle will be alive and well in every teaching context. Whether it is a calculus, organic chemistry, or anthropology class, teachers and students will teach writing and use writing to learn.

Essential #2: Writing Is a Process

The good news about a process is that everyone is skilled at some part of the process. Find and celebrate student strengths. Nobody is good at everything when they start, and failure is part of the fun. Teach students to use their failures as a path to success. Help them to overcome any affective filter that may exist because of past negative writing experiences. Students must be taught that nobody writes a good first draft. It is only through the process of revision, editing, and adding that a masterpiece can be created. Write the bad paper first. Writing is a process, not a product.

TRY THIS: Writer's Workshop

Host an 8-week writer's workshop in your class. Serve tea. Invite published writers to share their work. Guide students to the completion of a project by supporting them through the process of writing.

- Week 1: Brainstorming and Writing
- Week 2: Research, Reading, and Writing
- Week 3: Prewriting and Writing
- Week 4: Drafting and Writing
- Week 5: Revising, Editing, and Writing
- Week 6: Rewriting and Writing
- Week 7: Sharing, Feedback, and Writing
- Week 8: Beginning Again and Writing

Keep going through the stages of the writing cycle in a continuous and ongoing way. Coach students to learn that a piece of writing is never actually finished; it can always be better. Allow them to share and encourage each other along the way with an "open mic" reading opportunity. Allow them to talk through their ideas at each stage. Celebrate their efforts and bring in authentic audiences when you can. Writing is a process; enjoy the ride.

Essential #3: Writing Is Personal

Writing helps people process experiences. Because of the reflective nature of writing, writers can often experience pain, healing, and joy during the process. Keep this in mind as you guide your young writers. When they write something for you, read it. Be thoughtful, gentle, and compassionate even as you provide them necessary, critical feedback. Remember that when students trust you with their written work, they are trusting you with a part of themselves. Proceed with caution, but please proceed.

Writing and SEL

Writing can support students and teachers as they become more proficient in the areas of self-awareness and social awareness. Because writing is a personal journey of reflection, it can increase self-awareness in many ways. Writing allows teachers and students to identify and process emotions. Writing allows a teacher to consider his or her identity as an influencer of students in this unique area of communication.

For students, writing can be an avenue for self-awareness through reflection and emotional processing. The writing process can help students understand their strengths and needs and help them regulate how they spend their time. Writing is reflective and can be utilized as a way to process choices and make decisions. Specifically, teachers might use writing to help students identify problems and find evidence-based solutions. These problems and solutions could be academic or personal in nature.

Writing can also be used as a tool to manage stress. Consider adding journal writing to your self-care plan. Teachers and students can use writing to regulate emotions before reacting to emotionally charged situations. When taught well, writing can help teachers and students develop relationships through formal and informal communication.

TRY THIS: Letters of Encouragement

- Write a heartfelt letter to a parent discussing his or her child's hard-earned progress toward mastering a learning competency.
- Write a student an unsolicited letter of recommendation. In the letter, highlight the student's strengths and successes. Give it to the student to add to his or her portfolio.
- Using sticky notes, write a few short notes of encour-

You are a leader in the classroom, and I am thankful that you are here today.

I appreciated your thoughtful comment during the discussion today.

agement to distribute during a lesson. Communicate with students informally in writing throughout the day.

In Summary

Writing is a powerful force that requires time and effort to do well. When teachers think of themselves as writing teachers, they can teach the personal process of writing to students, increasing SEL competency along the way.

Discussion Questions

1. Discuss the importance of all teachers seeing themselves as writing teachers. What training do you need to feel more confident with this idea?
2. Think about a particularly challenging or difficult time that you have experienced. Did you use any writing strategies to get you through it, such as journaling, posting on social media, or writing letters? If so, what was the outcome? If not, which of these writing strategies might have helped you cope? How can you add writing to your self-care plan?
3. Think of one assignment that you plan to do this week in your classroom. How could you incorporate writing into your lesson plans?

Journal Prompt

Throughout this chapter, I compared the process of writing to running a marathon. What other activity or process could you compare to writing? Write a paragraph explaining how this activity is like writing. Have fun with this!

Bonus Writing Prompts for Students

Science: Do you have *biophilia* (*bio*—life; *philia*—love)? E. O. Wilson (1984) said that "Humanity is exalted not because we are so far above other living creatures, but because knowing them well elevates the very concept of life" (p. 22). Is this statement true? And if so, shouldn't every student love biology class?

Social Studies: The film *Won't You Be My Neighbor?* celebrates the life and career of Fred Rogers (Neville, Ma, & Capotosto, 2018). In this film, we hear Fred Rogers say that feelings are both mentionable and manageable:

> Anything that's human is mentionable, and anything that is mentionable can be more manageable. When we can talk about our feelings, they become less overwhelming, less upsetting, and less scary. The people we trust with that important talk can help us know that we are not alone.

Based on this quote, what are three ways that you can manage your feelings this week?

Math: Math anxiety is real. How might you help someone who is experiencing math anxiety about an upcoming exam?

Art: Not everyone agrees on the definition of art. What do you think makes something art? How would you analyze a painting to determine if it is art?

Social Justice: Think of a social issue that you are very passionate about. Now take the opposite view. Write an editorial supporting the opposition.

Breathing and Movement

I've got to keep breathing. It'll be my worst business mistake if I don't.

—Steve Martin

Take care of your body. It's the only place you have to live.

—Jim Rohn

It was 2013. I was working toward my 200-hour yoga teacher training certificate. I'll never forget my first assignment. It was simple, but it was not easy: *Get a partner. Watch her breathe.*

Seriously? I thought that I may have made a mistake. This was not what I had signed up for. Still, I got a partner, Michelle. I watched her breathe. In. Out. Up. Down. I watched the shape of her thoracic cavity change as her lungs expanded and contracted. I watched the slight movement of her face with each inhalation and exhalation. Life-giving oxygen entered in, and carbon dioxide went out. In with the good. Out with the bad. It was glorious. I was definitely in the right place.

Then it was my turn to be watched. As unnerving as it was, I found that having a stranger stare as I performed the most basic, involuntary life function was glorious, too. As I became aware of my own breath, I began to feel so much joy and gratitude toward this simple act. Breathing. Where would we be without it?

After we learned to breathe, we began to move. Over the next 18 months, I would learn the benefit of breathing and moving as a mindfulness practice in the yoga classroom. I would then learn that these methods can and should be incorporated into other classrooms as well. The fifth principle of mindfulness learning is Breathing and Movement. We will look at these parts one at a time.

Breathing

Breathing brings oxygen into the body. The oxygen travels into the nostrils, down the trachea, and into the lungs through the bronchiole tubes. Waiting in the lungs are tiny air sacs called *alveoli*, which are situated near capillaries, or tiny blood vessels. As the blood flows near the alveoli, the oxygen-rich atmosphere in the lungs creates what is called a *concentration gradient*. The oxygen sort of flows "downhill" into the bloodstream in the capillaries. The capillaries carry the blood to larger blood vessels that carry the now oxygenated blood to the heart. The heart's muscular chambers pump the blood to the entire body through the arteries. When the blood reaches the vital organs, such as the brain, stomach, and kidneys, a similar gas exchange occurs.

Then, when you eat, the body digests your food and breaks it down into the simplest form: glucose. The oxygen from the blood enables the mitochondria within your cells to convert glucose to the energy that you need to function. (*Note*. If you would like to read about these processes in more detail, please consult an introductory biology text. I recommend *Campbell Biology* [Reece et al., 2014].)

The point, as you may already know, is that breathing matters. Breathing is the fundamental biological process created to bring oxygen and nutrient-rich blood to each of our trillions of cells so that

Breathing and Movement

they can do their jobs. Amazing. The human respiratory system is a masterpiece. It works symbiotically with the human circulatory system and many other systems to give us life. Breathing is basic biology, but it is often taken for granted.

Consider the last time that you thought about your ability to breathe. Unless you suffer from asthma, or have seen or experienced severe respiratory illness, you probably don't think about it often. That's OK. That's how it is supposed to work. However, because we are working on paying attention, I'd like to call your attention to your breath. There is a reason that conscious breathing is the first thing you do during meditation. Conscious breathing has many benefits, which have their roots in biology, too.

Conscious Breathing: Biology 101

The former biology teacher in me is so happy to write this chapter; I'm literally dancing in my seat as I type these words. Conscious breathing activates your *parasympathetic nervous system* (PNS). This division of the nervous system is often referred to as the "rest and digest" system. When the PNS is activated, your heart rate slows, some of your muscles relax, and blood flow increases to some of your intestines and glands. Your body literally moves into a state of physical relaxation. This state reduces any anxiety. Relaxation via the parasympathetic nervous response is the exact opposite of stress. Who doesn't need less stress in their life?

Another direct and immediate benefit of conscious breathing and activation of the PNS is increased oxygenation of blood, which oxygenates the vital organs of the body. Consider the organ that we think about often in teaching and learning: the brain. When your brain is fully oxygenated and fueled, it can commence with full functioning. Specifically, an oxygenated brain improves mental clarity and focus.

The brain is not the only organ to benefit from deep, conscious breathing. Remember when I referred to the PNS as the "rest and digest" system? When your digestive system is fully oxygenated, it can work to break down your food so that your cells get the nutrients that they need to make energy. This allows you to stay awake and learn without feeling hungry, cloudy, fuzzy, lethargic, and all of the other ways that people feel when they are not being nourished. (This point also speaks to our need to support free breakfast and lunch programs at school.)

Conscious breathing and the parasympathetic nervous system also work to reduce the anxiety that gets in the way of learning. Consider the affective filter that goes up when students are attempting to learn in a high-stakes context. We know much about what this looks like in math and language learning.

TRY THIS: Conscious Breathing 101

* Before you begin your next cognitive task, such as making a decision, inhale a deep breath. Exhale. Repeat three times. Now, proceed. Reflect on your mental clarity and focus. This kind of conscious breathing also works well in the classroom, especially with language and math learning.
* The next time you are working with English language learners, draw their attention to their breath. This simple action will help them reduce anxiety before a new language task.
* The next time you are teaching math, reframe the math assessment using intentional conscious breathing as part of the preparatory process. A simple breathing activity can lower math test anxiety and consequently increase math performance (Alderman, 2016; Linden, 1973).

Attention to breathing increases oxygen levels and energy. Conscious breathing has multiple physiological and mental benefits: Overall mental functioning increases, anxiety and stress may decrease, and overall health may be influenced positively. Recent studies have found explanations for this phenomenon on a cellular and molecular level (Goldman, 2017; Yackle et al., 2017). With this scientific backing, there are no more excuses for not using this principle in your work.

TRY THIS: Reframe the Assessment

Before you distribute your next exam or high-stakes assessment, pause to breathe. Guide yourself and your students through a 1-minute breathing activity, consciously inhaling and exhaling 6–7 times. If possible, allow students to close their eyes as they breathe.

Every cell in your body needs oxygen and energy, and intentional breathing facilitates the process. Of course, I am not suggesting that you must always consciously breathe. Breathing, by design, is an involuntary process. You don't have to think about it, but if and when you do, you may increase the effectiveness and efficiency of its effects. So, what are the essentials of breathing as a principle of mindfulness?

Essential #1: Conscious Breathing Is Slow

I mentioned that conscious breathing arouses the parasympathetic nervous system, or PNS. The other system working in the autonomic nervous system is the *sympathetic nervous system* (SNS). The SNS is often referred to as the "fight or flight" system. The sympathetic nervous system is activated by the release of hormones, which cause physical reactions including opening of the blood vessels and increased heart rate. The SNS prepares your body for mental and physical work and can prepare the body for emergency response. When it is in full effect, the SNS increases sweating, heart rate, blood pressure, and breathing, and dilates the pupils. Blood flow is directed to the skeletal-muscular systems and diverted from some other vital organs (e.g., digestive system organs). When the SNS activates, you are ready to run (literally). This is wonderful and necessary and generally occurs in response to a temporary event. The SNS may save your life.

Mindfulness in the Classroom

The SNS is useful when it is needed. However, sometimes when you are under prolonged physical or emotional stress, your SNS works overtime for too long. This stress could be caused by environmental factors, like crowds and chaos, changes in routine, and high-stakes learning environments or exams. Hmm . . . sounds a bit like school to me. It is possible that merely being in school could activate the SNS of some teachers and students for prolonged periods of time. But the SNS isn't meant to be "on" at all times.

Thankfully, as you have learned, there is another part of the nervous system, the PNS, that can work to complement or address some of the physical effects of the SNS. One way to consciously address the body's physical reaction to stress is to activate the PNS with your breathing. Slowing down your breathing rate can cause a cascade of reactions that slow other functions down as well. If you are stressed, slowing your breath to a rate of six breaths per minute reduces it from the average adult's rate of 15 breaths or more. In turn, this slowing of the breath rate pumps the brakes and slows everything else. The heart rate slows, and the rest of the body calms down.

Consider the benefits for teachers and students. In the midst of a hectic day in the classroom, a teacher can stop and guide the class in six slow breaths. On the outside, only a minute has passed, but internally, calm takes over. Mental clarity and focus returns. Rational thinking and decision making result. Boom. Now, teach this trick to your students.

TRY THIS: Stop and Breathe

1. Tell students to close their eyes, place their feet firmly on the floor, and rest their hands gently in their lap.
2. Now, tell them to breathe in for 5 seconds. Count out loud: 1, 2, 3, 4, 5.
3. Tell students to exhale and breathe out for 6 seconds: 1, 2, 3, 4, 5, 6.
4. Repeat 10 times. Enjoy this moment. Enjoy this minute. Take a breather.

Breathing and Movement

Essential #2: Conscious Breathing Is Deep

Remember the "watch her breathe" experiment I mentioned at the beginning of this chapter? That was the first breathing exercise of many in my yoga instruction. Once we knew what breathing looked like, we tried it again. This time, we compared shallow and deep breaths. First, we observed shallow, thoracic breathing that begins in the nose and mouth and stops in the chest. Next, we watched one another as we breathed deeply, noticing how the belly moves as the breath is allowed to flow all of the way in and down. Conscious breathing is deep; you will notice that as you take your time with your breath, both your chest and your belly become full of rich, life-giving oxygen. This deep breathing takes longer, which, as we have already discussed, yields many benefits.

Essential #3: Conscious Breathing Is Rhythmic

We have spent some time discussing how your breathing can decrease anxiety and reduce stress via the PNS response. We have also discussed how important it is for this breathing to be slow and deep. What if you could engage in this kind of breathing consistently, steadily, and rhythmically? Conscious breathing, when done consistently, can produce a steady state of being in a person (Sima, 2014). Imagine how a rhythmic and steady flow of oxygen into your body would affect the steady production of energy in your cells. Rhythmic breathing can help your body to reach a state called *homeostasis*, a physical steadiness that can support a human's ability to achieve emotional stability. This stability can be beneficial for both teachers and students. Breathing isn't the only factor in achieving homeostasis, but it is an important component.

Think about your favorite Olympic swimmer, masterfully gliding through the pool and aligning each stroke with a well-timed breath. No pause is necessary. The swimming is rhythmic. Rhythmic breathing is something that swimmers must master to be at the top of their swimming game. So, what can we learn from swimmers?

TRY THIS: A Swimmer's Breath

With your students, pretend like you are swimming through the classroom. Model the freestyle swim stroke, rotating your arms one at a time: *Right stroke, left stroke, breathe on the right. Left stroke, right stroke, breathe on the left.* Alternate your breaths from the right to the left side. As you turn to breath, fully inhale, and as you return to your swimming motion, fully exhale. Repeat, counting rhythmically for students: *1, 2, breathe (on the right), 1, 2, breathe (on the left).*

Swim through the classroom together, practicing rhythmically breathing. If you have pool noodles, you might use those as props. Play the musical theme song from your favorite, marine-themed movie. I recommend "Beyond the Sea" from *Finding Nemo*. This is a fun way to practice rhythmic breathing. No pool required.

Breathing and Social Emotional Learning

For both teachers and students, conscious breathing supports self-awareness and self-regulation. When teachers and students become aware of their own breathing rate and style, they will begin to understand when it needs regulation. For instance, if a teacher knows that making a parent phone call or attending a faculty meeting tends to increase his anxiety, he can practice conscious breathing prior to the experience, elevating the PNS response and promoting a peace and calmness that will help him serve others well. For a student who has experienced stress in a learning situation in the past (e.g., during a standardized exam or before a speaking engagement), conscious breathing may decrease her heart rate and return blood flow to the digestive system and other vital organs, like the brain, enabling clear thinking and focus.

Movement

In the early 90s, there was a famous infomercial by a woman named Susan Powter (1993). Her famous catchphrase, "Stop the insanity," was followed by a tagline I'll never forget: "You have to eat, you have to move, you have to breathe." Movement and breathing (and eating) go hand-in-hand. You literally cannot move if your body doesn't have the energy resulting from the breakdown of food. Oxygen is required for this energy production. Clearly Susan Powter was onto something. Although I am not promoting her or any other weight loss program, I do want to spend a few pages discussing the second half of Principle 5: movement.

You have an amazing body. It is truly a miracle. Consider the way that your structural skeletal system is paired perfectly with a moving muscular system. In other words, you were born to move.

How have teachers traditionally used movement to facilitate learning in their classrooms? From my own observations: sparingly. Although we know of its importance, we have yet to capitalize on the amazing gift of movement as a tool to mindfully improve teaching and learning in our schools. Let's start today.

Remember when we discussed Principle 4, and I told you that you are a writing teacher, like it or not? Well, here's another newscast: *You must also teach students how to move.* They are going to move anyway. Trust me. And the younger they are, the more they will probably move. So, you, as the teacher, must teach them how. But first, consider why.

Why would you want to use movement in your classroom? Well, the obvious answer is to engage the hearts, minds, and bodies of your kinesthetic learners. But in addition to the benefits for these learners, moving improves brain function for everyone. Therefore, you want to use movement if you want to improve learning for everyone.

Research shows the connection between movement and mind function. Even short bouts of physical exercise improve cognitive functioning for children and adults (Tomporowski, 2003). Moreover, physical exercise also improves executive functioning with implications for increasing educational achievement outcomes (Davis et al., 2011).

Executive function of the brain includes the overarching functions and skills that help you receive and process information, including working memory, organization, and impulse control. Executive function enables us to pay attention, plan, prioritize, and regulate ourselves.

We have also learned from recent literature that exercise has benefits for students with Attention Deficit/Hyperactivity Disorder (ADHD), including improving specific executive functions, such as reaction times, which are related to impulse control and regulation (Benzing, Chang, & Schmidt, 2018). Ratey and Hagerman (2008) called the science of exercise and the brain "revolutionary." I agree. We have to move.

If moving improves information processing, then teachers would be remiss not to use movement in our classrooms. Given what we know about the role of breathing and oxygen for proper organ function, there is no denying the link between movement and the brain. For this reason, we must be more intentional about how we use movement in the classroom.

Beyond mental functioning, movement is associated with emotional well-being. For example, a daily running habit can have an antidepressant effect on the runner (Bjørnebekk, Mathé, & Brené, 2005). You've got to move; you've got to breathe. So, what are the essentials for movement as a mindfulness principle?

Essential #1: Move First

Movement in the morning or at the beginning of an activity is best. In yoga, there is a reason why the *asana*, or physical movement and body postures, usually comes before the meditation or mantra. The body prepares the mind. Move first. Then be still. For small children, moving first is essential, as it helps to dissipate nervous energy. It may be counterintuitive, but moving first actually helps students find a state of calm, increasing their focus and attention. Moving first also prioritizes this activity in your room, guaranteeing that it will get done rather than pushed to the end of the day, forgotten, or dismissed. Have you ever noticed that gyms are the most crowded with the fittest people in the wee hours of the morning? Trust me on this one and move first.

Essential #2: Move for Flexibility, Stability, and Strength

This sounds like three essentials, doesn't it? But I want to discuss the connection between these three concepts because, depending on your background or experience with sports, you may have a bias toward one or more of these attributes. All three are important, and all must be considered, taught, practiced, and developed.

I avoided yoga for years, thinking that I could never do it because I am not, and will never be, flexible like Gumby. When I finally found the right teacher, I learned that flexibility was only part of the game. Flexibility had to be balanced with stability, and stability required strength.

Using movement in your classroom is about helping students develop their flexibility, stability, and strength. That said, implementing this principle can be as simple as trying one of the following options:

> » Put on a 10-minute stretching or yoga video in the morning.
> » Pause a lesson to let students balance on one foot while counting to 10.
> » Allow students to sit on a balance ball instead of a chair.
> » Ask students to walk around the track as they recite a poem or define terms that they just learned.

Consider other ways that you can incorporate movement into your classroom program. Are there collaborative games or partner stretches that you could teach that would improve students' relationship-building skills or social awareness? Certainly, anytime you are asking students to mindfully move, you will want to debrief what they have done. You never want students to walk away thinking that all they did in class was play freeze tag. If the freeze tag was tied into a brilliantly planned lesson on social justice, tell your students. Help them understand the method behind your madness. Using movement might require a few moments of direct teaching, making explicit what students have just done and why. By the way, if you are using movement for movement's sake, that is OK, too. But as I have said before, most of these principles are meant to be embedded into what you are already doing rather than used as an "add-on" or "must-do." I am acutely aware of the precious and limited resource of time in our schools today.

TRY THIS: Brain Reboot

Use the following call and response with students:

Teacher: "Stop the . . ."
Students: "Insanity!"

Have everyone stop what they are doing and complete 10 jumping jacks, 10 burpees, or 10 squat jumps. Then, everyone should immediately return to their work.

This brain reboot will have to be practiced multiple times in order to work, but when it does, it will give students' brains an immediate and needed boost of oxygen, refocusing the class to the task at hand.

In Summary

Breathing and movement are essential principles to be used in the classroom. Attention to the body through movement and breath will help students regulate behavior, down to the cellular level.

Discussion Questions

1. Take a moment to notice your breath. Try to slow down your breathing rate to 6–7 breaths per minute using the 5-count inhalation, 6-count exhalation technique. Breathe using this

Breathing and Movement

conscious breathing technique for 1 minute. How do you feel? Discuss the physical experience of activating your parasympathetic nervous system.

2. What are some barriers to using movement in your classroom? Brainstorm proactive ways to address these barriers. Plan a "Move First" activity for tomorrow.

3. List the body systems mentioned in this chapter. Discuss how they all work together. Pause for a moment to reflect on what the human body is capable of.

4. Discuss how breathing and movement, when used together, can promote self-regulation for students in the classroom.

Journal Prompt

Commit to engaging in one breathing and movement activity daily before your workday. Move first. Try doing this for one week. Consider keeping a log of your daily progress by recording your activities in a journal or by logging them on social media. Reflect on how you feel afterward. Consider how engaging in this task improved your physical, mental, and emotional functioning throughout the day.

Gratitude

Don't forget to say, "thank you."

—My mom

Gratefulness is the key to a happy life that we hold in our hands, because if we are not grateful, then no matter how much we have we will not be happy—because we will always want to have something else or something more.

—Br. David Steindl-Rast

My son is 2 years old. He still loves milk above all other things, and when I hear his sweet voice calling to me, "Meeeeeeiiiilllllk, please Mommy," it melts my heart. I love it when my sweet little boy remembers to say "please." He grabs my hand and leads me to refrigerator to retrieve his milk. I hand it to him, and hear his sweet voice get sweeter: "Thaaank yoooou." He starts drinking his milk and is off to play with his monster trucks.

This happens all of the time now, and I am so grateful for that. The sweetness of his gratitude doesn't diminish, no matter how frequent. But I will never forget the magnificence of the first time. It was early in his speaking development, and he didn't have too many words in his repertoire. When I heard him say, "Thaaank yoooou, Mommmy," I cried.

What joy! I was so proud of my well-mannered, gratitude-filled child. I thought about it for a long time afterward. Where did he learn this? I hadn't yet explicitly taught him the language of manners. Of course, I was planning to, but for this early start, I must give him the credit.

He must have been paying attention, watching and listening to the adults' interactions around him. I am so glad that gratitude is what he learned. He is being raised in a culture of gratitude. The people in his life, children and adults alike, have been modeling gratitude since the day he was born. Gratitude breeds gratitude. For that, I am so thankful.

Now, this anecdote is in sharp contrast to what I experienced nearly 19 years prior during my first year of teaching. I'll never forget the advice that I was being given. I'm sure you have heard these suggestions before: "Don't smile until Christmas," "Let them know who is boss," "You can always get less strict, so start out tough," and, to my dismay, "Never say 'please' or 'thank you.'"

What on earth was going on? I will never forget the magnitude of that advice either. I couldn't believe my ears. Saying "please" and "thank you" was second nature to me, part of how I showed love to others and how I exhibited my humanity. It was part of my core and nonnegotiable; I would never take that advice. So, I didn't. I treated my students with grace, saying "please" and "thank you," and expecting them to do the same. This worked really well (after I finally learned their names, of course—remember that mess?). Anyway, showing gratitude matters, and it has greatly improved my relationships over the years.

Let us consider how the concept of gratitude can benefit students and teachers in schools. When we focus on teaching gratitude in schools, it is considered a habit of mind. Researchers study the benefits of teaching habits of gratitude to children. Many benefits of being thankful are also social-emotional learning competencies. For example, teaching gratitude increases a sense of well-being, which is a form of self-awareness. Teaching gratitude also improves relationship skills (Lambert, Clark, Durtschi, Fincham, & Graham, 2010).

There are four essentials related to gratitude that are relevant to SEL, teachers, students, and general human well-being. We will look at each of them. But first, let us look at a couple of definitions.

Definitions and Domains

Gratitude has been defined as an appreciation of something freely given, or an affirmation of a source of goodness (Gratefulness.org, 2018). The mental act of appreciating is important and has not been taught enough in schools. Let us consider another definition of gratitude: "Gratitude is an emotion or state resulting from an awareness or appreciation of that which is valuable or meaningful to oneself" (Lambert et al., 2010, p. 574).

Given these definitions, gratitude would fall into the affective domain of learning, a field of equal importance to cognitive learning. Traditionally, we focus less attention on the affective domain in schools. This area has been given less time and systematic attention. Let us consider why.

Why have some mental acts, such as appreciating or affirming, been given less attention in schools than other mental acts, such as remembering, classifying, or organizing ideas? We might find the answer with a look at Bloom's taxonomy. Traditionally, the cognitive domain has dominated the school curriculum. Using Bloom's taxonomy, we have focused on teaching thinking skills across the content areas (Krathwohl, 2002). These thinking skills have been organized into levels, and teachers write lesson objectives that address the development of thinking using this leveled system. For example, you might find content-specific lessons about remembering, understanding, applying, analyzing, evaluating, or creating.

The affective domain focuses on other skills and mental acts. Teaching in this area helps kids develop emotionally. Students who develop affective competencies learn to process emotions and respond appropriately given their social context. They learn to process feelings and understand values. They develop appropriate attitudes and appreciation for various subjects and ideas. Although it hasn't always been at the forefront of how we prepare teachers for service, recently there has been a renewed focus on the affective domain in many university-based and alternative teacher preparation programs. After years of neglect, with the publication of specific SEL competencies, as well as books like this one, this domain is garnering much-needed attention.

Unfortunately, there is still bad advice out there urging teachers to avoid using words like *appreciate* in lesson objectives, as appreciation cannot be measured. The misconception is this: If it cannot be measured, it should not be included in the lesson objectives, and if it is not an expected learning outcome, it will likely not be explicitly taught. In other words, it isn't on the test. But that is a conversation for another book.

For our purposes, let us consider how we might support students' development of "attitudes of gratitude." Let us consider how we can pay attention and observe growth in this area. Let the principle of gratitude matter, even if we are never accountable on a standardized state exam. Consider the opportunity to collect qualitative data to support the implementation of this principle.

TRY THIS: Mini Action Research Project

1. Before you implement any of the gratitude activities in this chapter, count the number of times that your students say "please" and "thank you" to one another in class. After you have implemented the activities, count the "pleases" and "thank yous" again. This simple exercise won't win you any prizes or get published in any scientific journals. However, it will provide evidence to justify continuing these practices in your classroom.

Gratitude

2. Instead of collecting quantitative data about gratitude, collect qualitative data. Observe individual and group behaviors before and after you teach gratitude habits to kids. Answer the following question in a journal or teaching portfolio: *How has implementation of the gratitude principle of mindfulness changed the climate of your classroom?* Use your senses to make detailed observations. Document your findings, analyze, and report any changes over time.

3. Use student journal entries to track development of "attitudes of gratitude" over time. Consider providing journal prompts that encourage students to think about the answers to the following questions:
   - How have gratitude-related activities helped you develop your awareness of how others affect you?
   - Are you becoming more aware of the good things and people in your life?
   - When you are thankful to others, how do your relationships change?

4. Use the qualitative data that you collect to make instructional decisions.

5. If you like, share the results with our teaching community by posting insights and findings on social media using #teachservelove. (For confidentiality, avoid using student names and identifying information when you share in the public domain.)

Remember, if you don't see change right away, do more modeling and explicit teaching about gratitude. Embed it into what you are already doing in your classroom. Then, just like my son, your students will become thankful and learn to appreciate goodness and gifts. They will learn that there are expectations and norms in the culture of gratitude that you have created, and they will adhere to those. Try it. Embed the principle of gratitude in a continuous cycle of instructional improvement, just as you would with any cognitive and academic task.

You will not be disappointed. You will see growth, and if you continue to collect qualitative data, you will be able to prove that growth. Here are a few essentials that will get you started.

Essential #1: Gratitude Is Simple

As I mentioned earlier, gratitude is a mental act, or a *habit of mind*. Once a habit is formed, it is simple to continue the behavior. There are some easy tasks that you can do daily that build the habit of gratitude.

TRY THIS: Daily Gratitude Habit

Every morning when you wake up, say, "Today I am thankful for
_____."

Set a reminder on your phone to do this. Say the words aloud if possible. This simple act of daily gratitude puts you into a positive mindset from the start.

TRY THIS: Thank-You Texts

Send a thank-you text to someone every afternoon. This message can be as simple as "Thank you for being you" or "Thank you for fixing my coffee this morning." Use an emoji. Start today.

When you exercise your gratitude habits daily, you are making deposits into a "thank" account. You are building a base of positive affirmations and affiliations that you can draw upon later when you need to remember what is good in your life. If you have an accumulation of positive memories and thoughts, it may help you regulate your emotions on days when you feel blue.

Gratitude

Along with building daily habits of gratitude, there are other habits worthy of building into your life and into your classroom.

TRY THIS: Week of Gratitude

Here are five weekly gratitude habits that you can use either alone or with your students to build a culture of gratitude in your world.

Monday: Gratitude Greetings. Check in with your students on Monday morning with a greeting of gratitude. Thank them for being with you. Share a story of gratitude or something that you are thankful for, perhaps a story of something that happened over the weekend. Give students some time to share gratitude stories of their own.

Tuesday: Thank-You Notes. Stock up on thank-you notes from the dollar store. On Tuesday morning, allow your students to write thank-you notes to someone. You can have a weekly theme for this activity. Some people to thank include family members, strangers, school employees, first responders, military service members, and community helpers. This is a wonderful weekly writing assignment for students in second grade and older. If your students are younger than second grade, they can draw their thank-you notes. If you teach emergent writers and English language learners, consider using a sentence frame and allowing them to fill in the blanks:

Dear _____ ,
Thank you for _____ .
Love, _____ .

Wednesday: Gratitude Wall of Fame. Create a place in your room for thanksgiving. This could be a bulletin board where you post pictures of people or stories about gratitude. Each Wednesday, add to the Gratitude Wall of Fame.

Thursday: Thankful Thinking. On Thursday mornings, do a 1-minute thought experiment. Think about what you are thankful for that day. Take six full breaths as you picture this thing in your mind. This gratitude activity also supports Principle 5: Breathing and Movement. Deep, conscious breathing will activate your parasympathetic nervous response, and allow you to relax into your thankful thoughts.

Friday: Gratitude Journals. In your journal, write or draw three things that made you smile throughout the week.

If you consistently practice these simple acts of gratitude, you will change your mindset. There is always something to be thankful for. There is always a reason to smile.

Monday	Tuesday	Wednesday	Thursday	Friday
Gratitude Greetings	Thank-You Notes	Gratitude Wall of Fame	Thankful Thinking	Gratitude Journals

Essential #2: Gratitude Builds Health

There is evidence that experiencing gratitude leads to perceived improvements in psychological well-being A study of 1,600 participants (Emmons & McCullough, 2003) indicated that keeping a gratitude journal had positive effects on physical health as well. People who practice gratitude reported more positive emotions than average. Thankful people also reported high resilience to stress and heavy workloads. We need more research in this area, but initial results indicate that expressing gratitude has many positive outcomes, including building emotional and physical health

Essential #3: Gratitude Brings Joy

Try thanking someone without smiling. I'm sure it can be done, but it is a bit of a challenge. Gratitude really does bring joy, both to the giver and receiver. This is huge because joy is the key to a happy life. A quick distinction: Joy and happiness are not the same. The glorious thing about joy is that it can exist even during hard or sad times. Joy is a good feeling in the soul that can come from being thankful.

Essential #4: Gratitude Improves the Strength of Relationships

When you step out and offer gratitude to someone, you are connecting with that person. In fact, when gratitude is involved, you are not just making connections; you are making *strong* connections (Algoe, 2012). Gratitude acts as a great facilitator of social interactions, building trust and improving the strength of relationships. Algoe (2012) called this approach the "find-remind-and-bind theory," in which gratitude is more than merely a response to a benefit received. Gratitude helps a person to "find" new relationships or to be "reminded" of old, significant relationships. The gratitude event binds that person to another, psychologically strengthening the relationship. If it is true that gratitude builds and solidifies important relationships in our lives, then I would say we have both a social and a moral responsibility to teach kids how to offer gratitude. Consider posting a banner that says "Gratitude: find-remind-and-bind." Teach your students what it means.

Gratitude and SEL

Gratitude is important for individual well-being and social interactions. As people begin to understand what they are thankful for, habits of gratitude help individuals become self-aware. When we thank others, we become more socially aware, too. Practicing a daily habit of gratitude helps us self-regulate our mood and perceptions of well-being. Extending gratitude helps us become aware of the goodness that we receive from others. Gratitude builds relationships and the social capital that students need in order to be successful in life. Let us practice it daily and add it into our lessons as often as we can.

In Summary

In the spirit of gratitude, thank you for everything that you do as a teacher. I truly appreciate you and honor what you do for schools and society. I have so much gratitude in my heart for teachers that I wish I could buy you all a present. Instead, my sincerest gratitude will have to do.

Discussion Questions

1. Consider a time in your life when you were immersed in a climate of gratitude. How did you feel? What habits were being practiced? Which of these habits can transfer into your work in schools? If you have never been in a climate of gratitude, then what habits will you cultivate now to create one for yourself and your students?

2. Think of one person in your life whom you want to thank. Plan a gratitude retreat for this person. This retreat could be a simple coffee outing or a more elaborate weekend getaway. How will you thank this person for what he or she does? If possible, make the retreat plan a reality.

Gratitude

Journal Prompts

1. Consider the relationship between gratitude and joy. At what time in your life did you feel authentic joy? What was the role of gratitude during that experience?
2. Think of a physical item that you love. If you could thank the person who invented this item, what would you tell him or her? How has the item made your life better? Write the inventor a note or make a video. Thank the inventor for this contribution to the world and to your life. (The inventor can be living or not; the act of gratitude matters here.)

Holding Space

Sometimes the hardest thing about holding space is that it can feel like you are doing nothing.

−Anonymous

Really listening and suspending one's own judgment is necessary in order to understand other people on their own terms ... This is a process that requires trust and builds trust.

−Mary Field Belenky

I was first introduced to the notion of holding space when I volunteered at a summer art camp for kids in Austin, TX. The individuals who volunteered as classroom teachers were never called teachers. Instead, they called themselves and one another "space holders." At first, I didn't understand what that meant. But when I saw my name listed as "space holder" for the 9–10-year-old students, I knew I needed to figure it out.

 DOI: 10.4324/9781003236665-12

A Definition of Sorts

Although it was never formally explained, I concluded that holding space was a beautiful metaphor for what was happening in the classroom. When the teachers held space for the students, the power differential disappeared, along with the labels of "teacher" and "student." Kids became teachers, and adults became learners. But the adults "held the space," allowing teaching, learning, and growing to occur. What I learned that summer, and the few summers that followed, was more than the definition; I learned the importance of holding space for the adults and kids in our lives.

Holding space is described as "a conscious act of being present, open, allowing, and protective of what another person needs in each moment" (Brady, 2019). Holding space is an art that requires you to know when to offer insight, when to suspend judgment, when to listen empathetically, and when to do nothing at all. Holding space is about being present with others. It is walking and sharing life experiences with people step-by-step. Holding space is not a passive activity, as it might seem. The space holder is an active participant and observer in the process. Much like a teacher or facilitator, the space holder is essential for learning, with one major difference: The space holder relinquishes the need to control.

A Tale of Two Spaces

During the time when I was a space holder in one program, I was also teaching in a very regimented, standards-based program on the other side of town. Each afternoon, I would leave the space that I was holding and go to a classroom where the state was driving the curriculum and the teachers were driving the students. In one situation, exploration and freedom were encouraged and even expected. In the other, no deviation from the set course was allowed or tolerated. What a dichotomy to behold. I learned the value of both approaches, noting that each system came with various pros and cons.

Holding Space

Not all kids thrived in either situation. But all kids could benefit from both. What if we could embed the principle of holding space into a more traditional and regimented program, using it when it was needed and thereby relinquishing the need to control every second of every day?

A disclaimer: Classrooms need teachers. Teachers must facilitate learning and manage student needs, expectations, and behaviors. I am not advocating against teachers as classroom managers. Teachers must find a way to maintain safety and guide students down a predestined path. Teachers must be in control much of the time.

I am suggesting that holding space allows students to be themselves and explore the world. With you holding space for them, they can safely test boundaries and test authority. They can become the independent thinkers and creators they were born to be. Holding space offers students an autonomy that they rarely get and desperately need.

Balancing Act

Remember, this book is about paying attention. Paying attention allows us to understand when we need to step into a certain role. Practicing mindfulness allows us to recognize when we need to facilitate and when we need to pause and hold the space. When we are mindful, we will know when our students are ready to take ownership and sit in the driver's seat of their own learning adventure.

The practice of holding space requires a balance of holding on and letting go. This is a difficult act, and one that has not been practiced in school contexts often. The key to finding this balance is trust. As teachers, we must learn to trust ourselves and our students. We must trust ourselves to know when we have taught students well. And we must trust students to take what we have taught and move forward.

Teachers must hold the space for the balancing act of learning and be ready to catch students when they fall. Teachers can flow from one role to another, meeting students where they need to be met, and leading them where they need to go.

Teachers: Trust yourself to know what to do. Trust your students.

For a few beautiful years, I taught at a public charter, college preparatory school. During my first week there, I assigned my AP Biology students tons of homework. I graded their work with a fine-tooth comb, carefully marking and correcting each error with my red pen. My students were mortified. Two of them came to me, earnestly asking why I didn't trust them. I had not "held the space" for their learning. I had not given them any time or space to develop efficacy in learning biology. I had used my red pen to obliterate their confidence and their trust in me as their leader.

During my first weeks at this new school, my students taught me many lessons. They taught me to trust them and they held space for me as I attempted to understand a new school culture. They walked with me, suspending judgment. They became my teachers. And, when the time was right, I became theirs.

TRY THIS: Circle of Trust

Invite 6–8 students whom you trust to participate in a group discussion about learning and school. Allow them to sit in a circle, facing one another. Hold the space for them as they discuss their experience in learning at school. Listen. Allow them to process emotions, values, and conflicts. Try to suspend judgment. Avoid trying to fix their problems. Rather, listen and learn. Practice your role as the space holder.

Note. Don't allow this to become a venting session where other teachers and students are attacked or ridiculed. You, as the space holder, have a responsibility to create a climate of trust, compassion, empathy, and learning. If necessary, resume your role as the teacher-on-record and intervene.

Holding Space and SEL

Holding space is one of the more abstract principles. However, there are connections between mindfully holding space, teaching SEL competencies, and creating a positive classroom climate. I have articulated these connections in the following essentials.

Essential #1: The Space Belongs to Them (and You . . . but Mostly Them)

My mom and dad have a favorite saying: "Fly, little birdies." They use this phrase to encourage my brother and I to be more independent. This tactic has proven useful at certain critical junctures in our lives.

"Fly, little birdies." Isn't this the goal? Don't we want our children (and students) to be able to leave the nest and successfully spread their wings? Of course, we do. We do not want them in our homes, basements, or classrooms forever. We want them to own their knowledge and lives and fly. So, we must give them the freedom to try. We must be aware that independence is the goal.

Hold the space for them to grow so that they can *go*. The space belongs to them. And in this space, you are present, circling, protecting, and catching them if they fall. In this way, naturally, the space belongs to you, too. But mostly, it is the students' educational experience; the space belongs to them.

Gradual Release of Responsibility

So, how can we trust our students to do what they need to do? We are their teachers. We teach them what to do. We stand by them, holding the space as they try and, most likely, fail. But then, they keep trying. With our gentle and nonjudgmental presence, eventually they will get it right. There can be a gradual release of responsibility from teachers to students. Holding space is a kind of scaffolding that can be removed or extended as needed. This is where your professionalism and expertise are needed. Consider all of the tools that you have at your disposal to determine students' learning needs. Think about the assessments that you are already using. How can those assessments and other assessments inform you? What metacognitive assessments can you add to increase students' self-awareness of where they need your support?

TRY THIS: Three Questions

Use this simple metacognitive assessment task during which you ask your students what they need and how you can help. This task can be a formal writing assignment or an informal conversation. The key is to ask students three questions. Their answers or lack of answers will inform your practice. Use the information that they share to help you to determine what other questions to ask and how you can hold space for them as they learn. Ask them the following three questions:

1. How's it going?
2. What do you need?
3. How can I help?

Essential #2: Holding Space Occurs Within a Positive Classroom Environment

The abstract idea of supporting students and walking alongside them nonjudgmentally happens in the context of a positive classroom environment. This is an environment that the classroom teacher intentionally creates. Ideally, students are also involved in the process of creating this environment. There are many ways to create a positive classroom environment (MacSuga-Gage, Simonsen, & Briere, 2012).

I recommend applying brain biology as you create a space for learning. Here are some of my favorite tips:

Holding Space

>> Use calming smells to lower anxiety. Lavender and eucalyptus sachets or candles are my favorite.

>> Use color. Use calming colors in some areas of the room (blues and greens) and energizing colors in other areas (oranges, reds, purples). Use complementary color schemes (e.g., orange and blue) to create an aesthetically pleasing space.

>> When possible, arrange furniture into inviting clusters that promote intellectual dialogue and team work.

>> Create an environment that is text-rich. Build your classroom library to include books that relate to both the content you teach and the values that you want to instill. Post both content-related (e.g., the periodic table) and value-related (e.g., motivational quotes) text on the walls of your classroom. Display student work. Use text intentionally in your environment to teach and to inspire.

>> Consider your students with sensory needs. Do not overstimulate them by overdecorating.

>> Use natural elements when possible (e.g., plants, rocks, water elements).

>> Personalize some part of the room. The physical environment of the classroom should be an extension of you and what you are representing as their teacher.

Essential #3: Holding Space Is an Art

Teaching is an art and a science. When I think about teaching tasks, I visualize an art-science continuum. I reflect on where each teaching task might fall on the continuum. Is it more of an art or more of a science? From there, I gather my resources and execute a plan for implementation. Many tasks in teaching are both an art and a science.

For me, holding space falls onto the artistic side of the spectrum. It is a beautiful practice, but, like most artistic endeavors, it requires practice and grace. It will take time for you to master, and you will make mistakes. Keep trying. It is practice, not perfect.

Although more of a right-brained activity, holding space also complements the science of teaching and learning. The science supports the idea of creating a positive learning space as a way to promote creativity (Amabile, Barsade, Mueller, & Staw, 2005).

We know that we must teach the whole child. We know the importance of teacher efficacy and the teacher-student relationship. The principle of holding space supports what we already know to be effective teaching practice. Holding space is a mindful way of supporting students' autonomy as they develop in cognitive and affective learning domains.

In Summary: The Container

I love the concept of holding space. I think about this principle as the container that holds the other principles. I envision a space in which SEL competencies are developed. This space is a combination of the physical and emotional spaces where learning occurs. Mindful teachers intentionally build both by tending to the creation of a positive physical space and a safe emotional space. In this container, people can intentionally work on self, social, and relational skills.

Discussion Questions

1. Define the concept of "holding space." Has anyone ever held space for you? How did it help?
2. Do you trust students? How do you show your students that you trust them?
3. What are some elements of a positive classroom environment that you use?
4. Discuss the idea of a "gradual release of responsibility." How important is scaffolding in your classroom? How does your classroom environment show evidence of scaffolding?

Holding Space

Journal Prompt

Holding space has been described as the gift of "presence." Think about a typical day in the classroom. How do you stay present amid the chaos of the day? If you don't, commit to being present with your students tomorrow. Find at least one moment during the day in which you enjoy merely being with them, enjoying them for who they are and what they bring to the classroom space. Write about that experience. How can you create more moments of presence?

Commit-to-One

Be faithful in small things because it is in them that your strength lies.

—Mother Teresa

The kind of commitment I find among the best performers across virtually every field is a single-minded passion for what they do, an unwavering desire for excellence in the way they think and the way they work. Genuine confidence is what launches you out of bed in the morning, and through your day with a spring in your step.

—Jim Collins

Every August, and sometimes in July, I start to hear the buzzing of the teaching force. Teachers everywhere are beginning to think about, dream about, and prepare for their upcoming school year. Sure, there is sometimes the occasional grumble or lament as the end of summer draws near. But mostly, teachers feel excitement and anticipation about meeting their students and being the best teachers they have

 DOI: 10.4324/9781003236665-13

ever been. There is something quite extraordinary about being in a profession that allows you a clean slate every new term. You get to start over, you get to try new things, and you get to be better than you once were. Starting over is a wonderfully refreshing experience.

Starting over is also hard. Each new school year, it is a bit daunting to know that the highly skilled and trained students you taught last year won't be waiting for you on Monday morning. Instead, you will have fresh faces, but you also have to start at the beginning with them. Correction: You *get* to start at the beginning with them. This realization, be it wonderful or sobering, is a reality of the teaching profession, one that requires guts and commitment.

Commitment is passion and dedication to staying the course. Without knowing what to expect, teachers show up and try again. I love this about teachers. I love a teacher's committed heart. Commitment is the final principle on this mindfulness journey.

Two Steps to Success

Today, my house is neat and tidy. This is quite a feat considering that I have a toddler running around with peanut butter on his fingers. It is also quite a feat considering that cleaning has never really been my forte. Seriously, you should have seen my closet in college. Yikes! But I'm getting better in my older age, and I think it is because I stick to two simple rules:

» Do just one thing.
» Finish that thing.

That's pretty much the key to anything. Pick one thing. Do it. Finish it. Then do the next thing. Finish that thing. Rinse and repeat.

For those of us who take an all-or-nothing approach to doing things, the reality of having so many choices can be daunting. It doesn't have to be. Just like my rules for tidiness, you can start with doing just one thing and finish that thing. It works. Trust me; that is why I don't have dishes overflowing in my sink anymore. That is how

I wrote this book. One piece at a time. Try it. You will not be sorry. Commit-to-one.

The good news about the commit-to-one approach is that it is only one thing. If it fails, fine. Try something else. If it succeeds, fantastic! Try something else, too. Committing to one thing will not make or break your teaching career. You can start anytime. Is it August and you have a million other things on your list? No problem—just try one more. Is it February and you feel like you need to start over again? Perfect. Start with just one thing. Finish that thing.

TRY THIS: Commit-to-One Activity

Return to Principle 1: "I" Work. Skim through the chapter, noting the "Try This" sections. Pick one thing. Commit to trying this one thing.

Say aloud, "I will commit to _____." Tell a friend. Now, go try it. Finish it.

Committing to one thing is the only way to accomplish goals. Reading and talking are great preparatory activities, but then you must do something. You will never regret and can always learn from trying. Trying leads to commitment. There are four essential ideas that I want you to remember about commitment.

Essential #1: Commitment Shows What You Believe

There are several common expressions and old adages (read: clichés) that illustrate this essential (e.g., "talk is cheap" and "actions speak louder than words"). But let us explore this essential further, especially in terms of committing to an idea that we, as teachers, implement in our daily practice

Mindfulness in the Classroom

Say What You Mean

Remember when you were in your original teacher preparation program and you were given the assignment to write your teaching philosophy? If you already did this, as most of us did, you might remember some of the things that you wrote. I truly hope that some of your ideals ring true today. Mine went something like this: "I believe that children are our future." Oh, wait, that's a Whitney Houston song . . . it actually went like this:

> I believe that *all* kids can learn. I believe that teachers can meet students where they are and take them where they need to be. I believe that teachers should teach the whole child, addressing academic, social, emotional, and physical needs. . . .

You get the idea. I didn't know it at the time, but my "I believe" statements were related to my strong commitment to equity and the teacher's role in whole child development as a way to pursue academic excellence. If you read my philosophy today, the language has matured, but the ideas are relatively the same. Here is the 2019 version:

> I stand in front of my students each semester and say, "Teaching is not what I do; it is who I am." I believe that. Teaching is my calling and my gift. I must do it well. Teachers and their students must find a way to succeed. As a teacher, I influence people's lives daily, significantly affecting life journeys, sometimes without knowing when or how. What I do matters in the world. Teachers have a particularly special moral responsibility.
>
> I teach to inspire my students to acknowledge their gifts and fulfill their potential in this world. I teach *all* of my students, meeting them where they are and taking them where they want and need to be. After 19 years in this business, I remain hopeful about the possibilities of education, even as I know the realities of the current system of schooling in our nation. I have seen the power of a social justice-oriented

education. Educators can transform the lives of individuals, schools, and communities. I know what high expectations for all students can do. I understand the necessity of rigorous curriculum. I also know that a rigorous curriculum only works with the nurturing scaffolds needed for students to access it. This curriculum works best on a campus with strong administrative and teacher leadership and a consistent, college-going culture.

I believe in developing social capital on a campus through relationships with students, families, and communities. I also hope to develop cultural capital in my students, so that they may understand and learn to appreciate the tastes and values of others. I integrate real-world experiences and examples when possible, bringing learning to life.

I believe in using a mindfulness framework to support the development of social and emotional competencies for both teachers and students. Specifically, I believe in embedding mindfulness principles into the daily work of teaching and learning. These include a focus on identity, integrity, and inspiration, creativity, building connections, using writing, practicing gratitude, holding space for learning, committing to trying new things, and breathing through the challenging moments.

When done well, teaching can be an avenue for ending oppression and increasing opportunity. My hope is that all teachers might be empowered with this understanding. Effective teachers weave the science of teaching together with their own artistic or creative strengths. They do this with grace, modeling expertise and exhibiting vulnerability coupled with courage.

TRY THIS: Write (or Revise) Your Teaching Philosophy

Answer the following questions about your teaching practice. Do this openly and honestly. Once you have answers in mind, write a 1–2-page narrative entitled "My Teaching Philosophy."

Think about your current understandings and definition of teaching and learning. What do you believe is the purpose of education? What is the teacher's role in achieving that purpose? What does effective teaching look like? What methodologies and practices do you believe work? Why do you teach?

Do What You Say

OK, so that teaching philosophy I shared is great, right? A philosophy with some powerful academic language ("teacherese," if you will), it looks good attached to my resume, too. But what happens if I never *do* anything with the words? Words are meaningless without the action of commitment behind them. So, what would my commitment to these words look like? What should I be doing to show the world, my school, my boss, and my students that I really believe the things that I say in my philosophy? A few key themes ring out when you read my philosophy, including:

- » social justice/equity,
- » finding ways to help *every* student succeed,
- » rigorous curriculum,
- » mindfulness,
- » social and emotional learning,
- » strong leadership,
- » social capital,
- » scaffolding,
- » creativity,
- » courage, and
- » developing gifts and strengths.

So, if I espouse these ideals, then what would you expect to see when you walk into my classroom? You would likely expect to see collaborative work, with students practicing and showcasing their strengths. All students would be engaged in critical thinking and rigorous coursework regardless of their special needs. Many different learning and teaching strategies would be utilized to support learning. There would be activities that are outside-of-the-box, and you would see me courageously trying new strategies and methods. As a teacher leader, I would be helping other teachers try new things also. In areas in which I felt weak, I would be seeking out other people in leadership for support. In order for my philosophy to bear fruit, I need to enact the things that I say that I believe in. This is commitment. It is committing to what I believe and taking action. Commitment matters.

Essential #2: Commitment Shows What You Value

When you commit to doing something of value, it typically requires an allotment of resources. In the field of education, the most precious of those resources are time and energy. Trying something new in the classroom takes time. Time is required to research, prepare, implement, evaluate, and reflect on the new strategy, method, etc. We, as educators, will not try something new unless we have found it to be a valuable use of our limited time and resources. Therefore, committing to one thing indicates that you value that thing. When you commit to any of these mindful practices—"I" work, creativity, cultivating connections, writing, breathing and movement, gratitude, holding space, or commit-to-one—you are showing that you value mindfulness and all of the fruit that it will yield.

The fruit of mindfulness in the classroom is social and emotional development for the teacher and the student. It is helping people become more aware of themselves and how they interact and contribute in the social contexts in which they serve. Attention to the essential elements of each principle has potential to elevate humanity and improve academic performance. It could even increase test scores, if that is what you are after. What do you value? Do those things.

Essential #3: Commitment Opens Doors

Lately I've been thinking about how "big" stuff happens. How do revolutions begin? How do we make great change where change is needed? We have to start somewhere. As I continue my work in education, I have noticed that sometimes I have to take the first step toward the closed door *before* it opens. Commitment can open that door. Commitment is motivating. Commitment means progress toward a goal.

Consider the common experience of a novice in any field. He or she has a dream job in a dream location and has done some of the preliminary work toward attaining that goal. However, when he or she applies, the company says, "Come back after you get some more experience." A committed individual will not let that closed door stop him or her, but will take steps to get the needed experience before trying again. The door will eventually open, and his or her efforts will be motivated by that knowledge. Commitment means progress, and progress is motivating.

Essential #4: Commitment Leads to Success

Desire is the key to motivation, but it's determination and commitment to an unrelenting pursuit of your goal—a commitment to excellence—that will enable you to attain the success you seek.

—Mario Andretti

Commit-to-One

Finally, commitment leads to success. If you've seen any of those motivational posters around your campus, you may have read something about that a time or two. But, let's revisit that statement mindfully. Think about it: You cannot achieve the things that you want to achieve without commitment. This is a very simple concept, but it is essential. It really comes back to the two steps: picking the one thing and doing the one thing. Both require commitment. Commit-to-one and commit to following through until it is finished.

TRY THIS: Commitment Wall

Post commitment statements on a wall in your classroom, and then honor those commitments by posting pictures of teachers and students as they do what they say they will do. This wall will become a wonderful, positive visual reminder of what you and your students believe and value, as well as what motivates you to succeed.

Commitment and SEL

Committing to something can support the development of self-efficacy and increase self-confidence. Consider the courage that it takes to start a task. For many people, starting a task requires the belief that completing the task is possible. This is self-efficacy (Bandura, 1982), and committing to just one idea or task can be a huge step toward developing the self-efficacy to complete a larger project. Consider how beneficial it would be if you had a mentor, facilitator, or teacher to support you in this process. Commit-to-one also allows you to work on achieving a goal in bite-sized chunks. We know that this approach, often seen in scaffolding of activities for students, is a way to develop students' confidence. This method of developing self-efficacy and self-confidence is transferrable to so many activities, academic and otherwise. It is applicable for both teachers and students.

Mindfulness in the Classroom

Commit-to-one enables teachers and students to develop in the areas of self-regulation. When you are committing to a task, you are typically setting goals and organizing a way to achieve those goals, one step at a time. This is practice in the area of self-regulation, and responsible decision making also plays a role in this process.

TRY THIS: Success Journal

Help your students develop a habit of daily journal writing as a way to record how commitments lead to success. Provide daily prompts related to learning goals. For example, if you are working with your students on developing their appreciation and commitment to reading, you could create a journal prompt like the one pictured below.

Success Journal

What did you read today?

_____

Circle the face that indicates how you felt about what you read:

Complete a journal entry summarizing what you read.

_____

_____

_____

Who will you tell about what you learned from your reading today?

_____

In Summary

Complete this sentence: To reach my goals for the upcoming year, I commit to doing _____ this week.

Good. Now go do it.

Discussion Questions

1. Consider the link between commitment and self-efficacy. What are some ways that you can encourage or promote students' belief in their own abilities?
2. Revisit your own teaching philosophy. Based on what you espouse, what should we see when we visit your classroom? What are you *not* doing that you need to commit to trying?

Journal Prompt

Consider a time in your life when you fully committed and accomplished a task. Now, think about the beginning of this experience. Can you recall how you actually made the commitment? Did you ease into the process in a series of baby steps, or was it one fateful leap, a decision that was immediate and life-changing? Either way, you had to commit and try one thing, right? How did this experience open doors? How did this accomplishment make you feel successful? What did this experience communicate to others about what you believe and value?

PART III

To Teach and Learn

Those who know, do. Those that understand, teach.

—Aristotle

In learning you will teach, and in teaching you will learn.

—Phil Collins

Today I taught. That is what I do. I am a teacher. It is part of my identity. It is a present that I open each time I step foot in a classroom. It is my gift, but not because I am good at it; it is a gift because I find joy as I unwrap the learning that lives in the carefully planned lesson. It is a life-giving pursuit that I choose to share with others. I don't feel this way every single class or every single lesson. Some days I sink under the weight of abominable failure. Some days I teach and then go home and cry. But those dark days of big and scary bumbles disappear in the light of a teachable moment. Let us not waste this gift we have been given.

 DOI: 10.4324/9781003236665-14

TRY THIS: Post a Quote

During the early days of my teaching career, I found the following quote. I mindfully posted it in my classroom as a daily reminder. Post this in your classroom. Watch the sun come out.

> I've come to a frightening conclusion that I am the decisive element in the classroom. It's my personal approach that creates the climate. It's my daily mood that makes the weather. As a teacher, I possess a tremendous power to make a child's life miserable or joyous. I can be a tool of torture or an instrument of inspiration. I can humiliate or heal. In all situations, it is my response that decides whether a crisis will be escalated or de-escalated and a child humanized or dehumanized.
>
> —Haim Ginott

A Call to Action

Twenty years from now you will be more disappointed by the things that you didn't do than by the ones you did do. So, throw off the bowlines. Sail away from the safe harbor. Catch the trade winds in your sails. Explore. Dream. Discover.

—H. Jackson Brown, Jr., *P.S. I Love You*

Action speaks louder than words but not nearly as often.

—Mark Twain

I cannot remember a time when I wasn't teaching and learning. I started playing "school" with my baby brother as soon as he could crawl. I played the teacher. When I was in elementary school, I volunteered to help my teachers whenever I could. As a high school and college student, I tutored my peers whenever they asked and sometimes when they didn't. I wanted to teach. Fast forward a few years to the 22-year-old standing in my first classroom, facing a group of freshmen in high school. I wanted to teach, but I needed to learn.

 DOI: 10.4324/9781003236665-15

Mindfulness in the Classroom

I held teachers and teaching in such high regard. I still do. In my mind, teachers are heroes, able to change the world. I believed that I could do it, and I assumed it would be easy. Boy was I wrong. I had a passion for teaching and learning, but as a new, idealistic teacher, the challenging realities of classroom life threatened to extinguish my flame.

I was called to teach, but I needed to learn. So, I did. I went to trainings. I went to professional development sessions. I went on teacher retreats. Eventually, I went to graduate school. I sought out master teachers and teaching colleagues who would make me better. I learned from so many amazing teachers. I learned about the realities of schools as social institutions and the real, generational challenges that teachers face. I learned about classroom procedures and color-coding everything. I learned about inequity and opportunity gaps. I learned methods and strategies supported by theories and research. I even did a bit of research of my own.

As I learned, realizations about the systemic challenges that we face would leave me in tears. I considered leaving the field altogether. It was an uphill climb. Did I have the ability to persist? This year, as I begin my 19th year of learning names and writing lesson plans, I'm learning that the answer is: I'm still learning. Whether I teach seventh-grade science, preservice teachers, preschool Vacation Bible School, or adult English as a Second Language, I still have so much to learn.

If you are called to teach, you are called to learn. Always. The call to teach is ultimately a call to the pursuit of lifelong learning. As teachers, we must be in pursuit of tools that will support our students as they learn. As the world changes, we change, too. As our students grow, so do we.

The Proposal—Revisited

Let's revisit the proposal I outlined in Part I. Initially, I defined mindfulness as the simple act of paying attention. As you now know,

A Call to Action

that there is more to it than that. Mindfulness includes intentionally developing our personal and professional identities and remaining consistent in how we use our strengths in our work. It is essential to know and utilize our strengths to become agents of positive change in ourselves and the world (Bandura, 2008). It is about understanding and revealing our identities to inspire the people we teach. Mindfulness is about knowing who we are and having the courage to use our strengths in the classroom. Mindfulness means self-awareness and attention to integrity.

Mindfulness is using our imaginations to envision our future selves. It is using this vision to support goal setting and responsible decision making. Mindfulness is about intentionally connecting with others and becoming more socially aware. Mindful teachers are empathetic, compassionate, and gentle in how they interact and build relationships.

Mindfulness is about using metacognitive tools, such as writing and conscious breathing. Mindful people use their bodies, breathing and moving, regulating their parasympathetic nervous systems and stress levels.

Mindful teachers tune in when others support their work, and they respond in gratitude. Mindfulness is being aware and knowing when to hold space and when to intervene. Mindfulness is knowing that one step forward leads to commitment and success.

Mindful practices promote SEL competency development in the classroom. When teachers use a mindfulness approach, SEL happens. Following the eight mindful principles will lead to more self-awareness, self-regulation, social awareness, relationship building, and responsible decision making. Mindfulness helps teachers, students, and others become more socially and emotionally competent. A culture of mindfulness transforms the learning environment, making spaces more positive and productive. Mindfulness matters.

In Summary: The Call

If you have been paying attention, you will have realized that this book is much more than a proposal; it is truly a call to action. It is a call for us to use a mindfulness framework to develop SEL competencies in learners. It is a call to support human development in a principled way. It is a call to notice and take action in your sphere of influence for good. It is a call to help students become aware, compassionate, responsible citizens of the planet. It is a call to use eight principles to promote healthy social-emotional development in people.

For the classroom teacher, this book is a call to do this work and to use the principles in ways that support what you are already doing in the classroom. It is a call to increase academic success using a holistic approach.

The teacher is the key to the implementation and success of this framework. This book is a call that the classroom teacher can answer. Mindfulness matters, but it must matter to the teacher. The teacher must feel empowered and make this envisioned framework a living and breathing reality. The teacher determines what happens with his or her students. The teacher is holding the lever of change. The teacher influences lives, making the world a little more mindful, one student at a time. The question is: Will you?

Discussion Questions

1. What is your first step in the implementation of the eight mindfulness principles?
2. What do you hope to achieve?

Journal Prompt

Think about your philosophy of teaching and learning. How do the eight principles align with what you believe? What will you do so that your beliefs and actions demonstrate integrity?

Imagining a
Mindful World

Let us remember: One book, one pen, one child, and one teacher can change the world.

—Malala Yousafzai

As I write this final chapter, a sense of deep gratitude and reverence washes over me. I hold teachers in such high regard. I count it my extreme privilege to offer any support to them as they dare to do the impossibly demanding work of teaching. I love being a small part of what you do, and I love you. Thank you.

I hope that in these pages you have found some inspiration, empowerment, and, most importantly, some ideas that you can use. I challenge you to step out of your comfort zone and try new strategies.

As you engage in the activities, lessons, discussions, and journaling offered in this text, imagine a mindful world. Imagine the opportunity to create a classroom full of socially and emotionally aware and competent citizens. Consider the ripple effects as your students become citizens of the world. What a wonderful world it could be.

Practice the Principles

There is a reason why it is called "yoga practice," not "yoga perfect." Practice is the key. My hope is that you will take these principles and practice them, committing to one at a time, in order to build a culture of mindfulness and SEL. Practice the principles; that is where you begin.

As you practice the principles for yourself and in community with your students, you will notice change. Many of the practical applications of the principles are simple. Some are easy. Most are external actions with tangible outcomes. Start with the external. Externalize the principles through practice, and you will begin to internalize the social-emotional competencies that they produce. This is how learning works. Externalize to internalize. You will notice change.

Change Is Good

What changes can we really expect? I've talked about using mindfulness to make better humans. But what does a better human look like? What are the expected learning results? What can we hope for if this mindfulness movement truly takes hold?

In my dreams, I imagine that better humans are people who care. They care about themselves and others and the world they call home. Better humans love one another, and they live out that love in action, compassionately responding to the problems in the world.

Better humans regulate their emotions, dealing with anger in nonviolent, nonharmful ways. They feel empathy. They listen. Better humans are self-aware, knowing how to use their strengths for the greater good. Focusing on strengths is essential for positive psychology and positive change in the world (Bandura, 2008). Witnessing positive change helps us remain optimistic in a hurting world. Optimism helps us keep hope alive despite adversity, which increases our efficacy and resilience and makes us even better humans.

Imagining a Mindful World

Better humans notice the needs of others before their own. They apologize when they are wrong. They learn names and make eye contact. They pick up trash. Better humans are honest and kind, obeying authority when authority is good, and questioning authority when necessary.

Better humans forgive and ask for forgiveness. Better humans try to be better. Better humans do the right thing when no one is watching. Better humans change the world.

References

Alderman, L. (2016). Breathe. Exhale. Repeat: The benefits of controlled breathing. *The New York Times*. Retrieved from https://www.nytimes.com/2016/11/09/well/mind/breathe-exhale-repeat-the-benefits-of-controlled-breathing.html

Algoe, S. B. (2012). Find, remind, and bind: The functions of gratitude in everyday relationships. *Social and Personality Psychology Compass, 6*, 455–469. https://doi.org/10.1111/j.1751-9004.2012.00439.x

Alvarez, D., & Mehan, H. (2010). Whole-school detracking: A strategy for equity and excellence. *Theory Into Practice, 45*, 82–89.

Amabile, T., Barsade, S. G., Mueller, J. S., & Staw, B. M. (2005). Affect and creativity at work. *Administrative Science Quarterly, 50*, 367–403.

Argyris, C. (1997). Learning and teaching: A theory of action perspective. *Journal of Management Education, 21*, 9–26.

Association of American Educators. (n.d.). *Code of ethics for educators*. Retrieved from https://www.aaeteachers.org/index.php/about-us/aae-code-of-ethics

Bandura, A. (1982). Self-efficacy mechanism in human agency. *American Psychologist, 37,* 122–147.

Bandura, A. (2008). An agentic perspective on positive psychology. In S. J. Lopez (Ed.), *Positive psychology: Exploring the best in people* (Vol. 1, pp. 167–196). Westport, CT: Praeger.

Becker, H. S. (2007). *Writing for social scientists: How to start and finish your thesis, book, or article* (2nd ed.). Chicago, IL: The University of Chicago Press.

Benzing, V., Chang, Y., & Schmidt, M. (2018). Acute physical activity enhances executive functions in children with ADHD. *Scientific Reports.* Retrieved from https://www.nature.com/articles/s41598-018-30067-8.pdf

Bjørnebekk, A., Mathé, A. A., & Brené, S. (2005). The antidepressant effect of running is associated with increased hippocampal cell proliferation. *International Journal of Neuropsychopharmacology, 8,* 357–368.

Blakeslee, S., & Blakeslee, M. (2007). *The body has a mind of its own: New discoveries about how the mind-body connection helps us master the world.* New York, NY: Random House.

Bolman, L. G., & Deal, T. E. (2001). *Leading with soul: An uncommon journey of spirit* (Rev. ed.). San Francisco, CA: Jossey-Bass.

Borman, G. D., & Dowling, N. M. (2008). Teacher attrition and retention: A meta-analytic and narrative review of the research. *Review of Educational Research, 78,* 367–409.

Bourdieu, P. (1986). The forms of capital. In J. G. Richardson (Ed.), *Handbook of theory and research for the sociology of education* (pp. 241–58). New York, NY: Greenwood Press.

Brady, A. (2019). Holding space: The art of being present with others. *The Chopra Center.* Retrieved from https://chopra.com/articles/holding-space-the-art-of-being-present-with-others

Bransford, J. D., Brown, A. L., & Cocking R. R. (2000). *How people learn: Brain, mind, experience, and school* (Expanded ed.). Washington, DC: National Academies Press.

References

Brown, K., Ryan, R., & Creswell, J. (2007). Mindfulness: Theoretical foundations and evidence for its salutary effects. *Psychological Inquiry, 18,* 211–237.

Brown, T. (2009). *Change by design: How design thinking transforms organizations and inspires innovation.* New York, NY: Harper Collins.

Cha, H. G., & Kim, M. K. (2016). Effects of mental practice on normal adult balance ability. *Journal of Physical Therapy Science, 28,* 2041–2043. doi:10.1589/jpts.28.2041.

Coleman, J. S. (1988). Social capital in the creation of human capital. *American Journal of Sociology, 94,* S95–S120.

Collaborative for Academic, Social, and Emotional Learning. (2005). *Safe and sound: An educational leader's guide to evidence-based social and emotional learning programs.* Chicago, IL: Author.

Collaborative for Academic, Social, and Emotional Learning. (2013). *CASEL schoolkit: A guide for implementing school wide academic, social, and emotional learning.* Chicago, IL: Author.

Collaborative for Academic, Social, and Emotional Learning. (2018a). *CASEL program guides: Effective social and emotional learning programs.* Retrieved from https://casel.org/guide

Collaborative for Academic, Social, and Emotional Learning. (2018b). *Core SEL competencies.* Retrieved from https://casel.org/core-competencies

Collaborative for Academic, Social, and Emotional Learning. (2018c). *History.* Retrieved from: https:/casel.org/history

Collaborative for Academic, Social, and Emotional Learning. (2018d). *What is SEL?* Retrieved from https://casel.org/what-is-sel

Cullen, M. (2011). Mindfulness-based interventions: An emerging phenomenon. *Mindfulness, 2,* 186–193.

Davis, C. L., Tomporowski, P. D., McDowell, J. E., Austin, B. P., Miller, P. H., Yanasak, N. E., . . . Naglieri, J. A. (2011). Exercise improves executive function and achievement and alters brain activation in overweight children: A randomized, controlled trial. *Health Psychology, 30,* 91–98.

Demi. (1996). *The empty pot.* New York, NY: Holt.

Denham, S. A., & Brown, C. (2010). "Plays nice with others": Social-emotional learning and academic success. *Early Education & Development, 21,* 652–680.

Destin, M., Vida, M., & Townsend, S. (2018). Thoughts about a successful future encourage action in the face of challenge. *Motivation and Emotion, 42,* 321–333

Dika, S. L., & Singh, K. (2002). Applications of social capital in educational literature: A critical synthesis. *Review of Educational Research, 72,* 31–60.

Durlak, J. A., Domitrovich, C. E., Weissberg, R. P., & Gullotta, T. P. (Eds.). (2015). *Handbook of social and emotional learning: Research and practice.* New York, NY: Guilford Press.

Durlak, J. A., Weissberg, R. P., Dymnicki, A. B., Taylor, R. D., & Schellinger, K. B. (2011). The impact of enhancing students' social and emotional learning: A meta-analysis of school-based universal interventions. *Child Development, 82,* 405–432.

Dweck, C. (2006). *Mindset: The new psychology of success.* New York, NY: Random House.

Educate Inspire Change TV. (2014). *I will spark the brain that will change the world – Tupac* [Video file]. Retrieved from https://www.youtube.com/watch?v=uijBebYpoto

Elias, M. J., Zins, J. E., Weissberg, R. P., Greenberg, M. S., Frey, K. S., Haynes, N. M., . . . Shriver, T. P. (1997). *Promoting social and emotional learning: Guidelines for educators.* Alexandria, VA: Association for Supervision and Curriculum Development.

Emmons, R. A., & McCullough, M. E. (2003). Counting blessings versus burdens: An experimental investigation of gratitude and subjective well-being in daily life. *Journal of Personality and Social Psychology, 84,* 377–389.

Everson, B. (1991). Vygotsky and the teaching of writing. *The Quarterly of the National Writing Project and the Center for the Study of Writing and Literacy, 13*(3), 8–11.

Folkman, S., & Moskowitz, J. T. (2000). Stress, positive emotion, and coping. *Current Directions in Psychological Science, 9,* 115–118.

References

Foundation for a Mindful Society. (2017). *Jon-Kabat Zinn: Defining mindfulness.* Retrieved from https://www.mindful.org/jon-kabat-zinn-defining-mindfulness

Frayer, D., Frederick, W. C., & Klausmeier, H. J. (1969). *A schema for testing the level of cognitive mastery.* Madison, WI: Wisconsin Center for Education Research.

Freire, P. (2000). *Pedagogy of the oppressed* (30th anniversary ed.). New York, NY: Continuum.

Gee, J. P. (2000). Identity as an analytic lens for research in education. *Review of Research in Education, 25,* 99–125.

Gibney, K. (1998). Awakening creativity. *ASEE Prism, 7*(7), 18–23.

Goldman, B. (2017). *Brain study shows how slow breathing induces tranquility.* Retrieved from https://medicalxpress.com/news/2017-03-brain-tranquility.html

Gratefulness.org. (2018). *What is gratitude?* Retrieved from https://gratefulness.org/resource/what-is-gratitude

Griggs, T., & Tidwell, D. (2015). Learning to teach mindfully: Examining the self in the context of multicultural education. *Teacher Education Quarterly, 42,* 87–104.

Heitin, L. (2011). Writing re-launched: Teaching with digital tools. *Education Week.* Retrieved from https://www.edweek.org/tsb/articles/2011/04/04/02digital.h04.html

Hooker, K. E., & Fodor, I. E. (2008). Teaching mindfulness to children. *Gestalt Review, 12,* 75–91.

Hughes, J. N., Cavell, T. A., & Wilson, V. (2001). Further support for the developmental significance of the quality of the teacher–student relationship. *Journal of School Psychology, 39,* 289–301.

Intel. (n.d.). *50 years of Moore's law: Fueling innovations we love and depend on.* Retrieved from https://www.intel.com/content/www/us/en/silicon-innovations/moores-law-technology.html

Jensen, E. (2005). *Teaching with the brain in mind* (2nd ed.). Alexandria, VA: Association of Supervision and Curriculum Development.

Johnson, B. (2016). Outstanding in your field: What it takes to be a great teacher. *Edutopia.* Retrieved from https://www.edutopia.org/blog/teacher-excellence-part-one-ben-johnson

Kabat-Zinn, J. (2003). Mindfulness-based interventions in context: Past, present, and future. *Clinical Psychology: Science and Practice, 10*, 144–156.

Kinman, G., & Grant, L. (2011). Exploring stress resilience in trainee social workers: The role of emotional and social competencies. *The British Journal of Social Work, 41*, 261–275.

Krathwohl, D. (2002). A revision of Bloom's taxonomy: An overview. *Theory Into Practice, 41*, 212–218.

Kucher, K. (2012). Preuss named top 'transformative' school in U.S. *The San Diego Union-Tribune.* Retrieved from https://www.sandie gouniontribune.com/news/education/sdut-preuss-named-top-transformative-school-us-2012may21-story.html

Lambert, N. M., Clark, M. S., Durtschi, J., Fincham, F. D., & Graham, S. M. (2010). Benefits of expressing gratitude: Expressing gratitude to a partner changes one's view of the relationship. *Psychological Science, 21*, 574–580.

Lenhart, A., Madden, M., Smith, A., Purcell, K., & Zickuhr, K. (2011). Teens, kindness and cruelty on social media sites: How American teens navigate the new world of digital citizenship. *Pew Research Center.* Retrieved from https://www.pewinternet.org/2011/11/09/teens-kindness-and-cruelty-on-social-network-sites

Linden, W. (1973). Practicing of meditation by school children and their levels of field dependence-independence, test anxiety, and reading achievement. *Journal of Consulting and Clinical Psychology, 41*, 139–143. http://dx.doi/10.1037/h0035638

MacSuga-Gage, A. S., Simonsen, B., & Briere, D. E. (2012). Effective teaching practices that promote a positive classroom environment. *Beyond Behavior, 22*, 14–22.

Mandela, N. (1995). Nelson Mandela's quotes about children. *Nelson Mandela's Children Fund.* Retrieved from http://www.nelson mandelachildrensfund.com/news/nelson-mandela-quotes-about-children

Mani, A. (2014). Centered with compassion: Journal writing as a mindful practice and healing tool. *The Mindful Word.* Retrieved

References

from https://www.themindfulword.org/2014/centred-compassion-journal-writing-mindfulness-practice-healing-tool

Marzano, R. J. (2007). *The art and science of teaching: A comprehensive framework for effective instruction.* Alexandria, VA: Association for Supervision and Curriculum Development.

McLeod, S. (1987). Defining writing across the curriculum. *WPA: Writing Program Administration, 11*(1–2), 19–24.

McLeod, S. (2018). Maslow's hierarchy of needs. *Simply Psychology.* Retrieved from https://www.simplypsychology.org/maslow.html

Medrano, M. (2017). *The power of mindful writing.* Retrieved from https://www.rtor.org/2017/04/04/the-power-of-mindful-writing

Mehan, H. (2012). *In the front door: Creating a college-going culture of learning.* New York, NY: Routledge.

Montgomery D., Mele C., & Fernandez M. (2017). Gunman kills at least 26 in attack on rural Texas church. *The New York Times.* Retrieved from https://www.nytimes.com/2017/11/05/us/church-shooting-texas.html

Moore, K. (2015). *Effective instructional strategies: From theory to practice* (4th ed.). Thousand Oaks, CA: SAGE.

Mosle, S. (2014). Building better teachers: Mastering the craft demands time to collaborate—just what American schools don't provide. *The Atlantic.* Retrieved from https://www.theatlantic.com/magazine/archive/2014/09/building-better-teachers/375066

Mussey, S. (2009). *Navigating the transition to college: First-generation undergraduates negotiate identities and search for success in STEM and non-STEM fields* (Master's thesis). Retrieved from ProQuest Dissertations Publishing. (UMI. No. 3355909)

Mussey, S. (2012). Changes in students' aspirations and conduct: The role of institutional arrangements. In H. Mehan (Ed.), *In the front door: Creating a college-going culture of learning* (pp. 91–114). New York, NY: Routledge.

National Writing Project. (2011). *Writing is essential.* Retrieved from https://www.nwp.org/cs/public/download/nwp_file/13766/NWP_trifold_final.pdf?x-r=pcfile_d

Neff, C. (1989). Scorecard. *Vault*. Retrieved from https://www.si.com/vault/1989/07/10/106780416/scorecard

Neville, M. (Producer, Director), Ma, N. (Producer), & Capotosto, C. (Producer). (2018). *Won't you be my neighbor?* [Motion Picture]. USA: Tremelo Productions.

Newell, J., & Nelson-Gardell, D. (2014). A competency-based approach to teaching professional self-care: An ethical consideration for social work educators. *Journal of Social Work Education, 50*, 427–439.

Newman, K. S., Fox, C., Roth, W., Mehta, J., & Harding, D. (2005). *Rampage: The social roots of school shootings.* New York, NY: Basic Books.

Palmer, P. J. (1998). *The courage to teach: Exploring the inner landscape of a teacher's life*. San Francisco, CA: Jossey-Bass.

Patterson, K. (2012). *Crucial conversations: Tools for talking when stakes are high* (2nd ed.). New York, NY: McGraw-Hill.

Pierson, R. (2013). *Every kid needs a champion* [Video file]. Retrieved from https://www.ted.com/talks/rita_pierson_every_kid_needs_a_champion/transcript?language=en

Powter, S. (1993). *Stop the insanity!: Eat, breath, move*. New York, NY: Gallery Books.

Ramsey, D. (2018). *3 leadership lessons from George Washington* [Web log post]. Retrieved from https://www.daveramsey.com/blog/3-leadership-lessons-from-george-washington

Ranganathan, V. K., Siemionow, V., Liu, J. Z., Sahgal, V., & Yue, G. H. (2004). From mental power to muscle power—gaining strength by using the mind. *Neuropsychologia, 42*, 944–956.

Ratey, J., & Hagerman, E. (2008). *Spark: The revolutionary new science of exercise and the brain*. New York, NY: Little, Brown.

Reece, J. B., Urry, L. A., Cain, M. L., Wasserman, S. A., Minorsky, P. V., Jackson, R., & Campbell, N. A. (2014). *Campbell biology* (10th ed.). Boston, MA: Pearson.

Rennick, J. (2015). Learning that makes a difference: Pedagogy and practice for learning abroad. *Teaching & Learning Inquiry: The ISSOTL Journal, 3*(2), 71–88.

References

Robinson, K. (2006). *Do schools kill creativity?* [Video file]. Retrieved from https://www.ted.com/talks/ken_robinson_says_schools_kill_kill_creativity?language=en

Ryoo, J. J., Crawford, J., Moreno, D., & McLaren, P. (2009). Critical spiritual pedagogy: Reclaiming humanity through a pedagogy of integrity, community, and love. *Power and Education, 1,* 132–14.

Schaefer, L., Downey, C. A., & Clandinin, D. J. (2014). Shifting from stories to live by to stories to leave by: Early career teacher attrition. *Teacher Education Quarterly, 41*(1), 9–27.

Schonert-Reichl, K. A. (2017). Social and emotional learning and teachers. *The Future of Children, 27*(1), 137–155.

Sherretz, C. E. (2011). Mindfulness in education: Case studies of mindful teachers and their teaching practices. *Journal of Thought, 46*(3–4), 79–96.

Sima, B. (2014). *10 health benefits of conscious breathing* [Web log post]. Retrieved from https://www.bobsima.com/10-health-benefits-conscious-breathwork

Sinek, S. (2009). *Start with why: How great leaders inspire everyone to take action.* New York, NY: Portfolio.

Stack, L., & Stevens, M. (2018). Southwest airlines engine explodes in flight, killing a passenger. *The New York Times.* Retrieved from https://www.nytimes.com/2018/04/17/us/southwest-airlines-explosion.html

TeachThought Staff. (2016). *A teacher makes 1500 educational decisions a day.* Retrieved from https://www.teachthought.com/pedagogy/teacher-makes-1500-decisions-a-day

Tobin, K. (2018). Mindfulness in education. *Learning, Research, and Practice, 4,* 1–9.

Tomporowski, P. D. (2003). Effects of acute bouts of exercise on cognition. *Acta Psychologica, 112,* 297–324.

University at Buffalo. (2018). *Developing your self-care plan.* Retrieved from https://socialwork.buffalo.edu/resources/self-care-starter-kit/developing-your-self-care-plan.html

University of Pennsylvania. (2018). *Creativity and imagination.* Retrieved from https://www.authentichappiness.sas.upenn.edu/learn/creativity

Vygotsky, L. S. (1978). Interaction between learning and development. In M. Cole, V. John-Steiner, S. Scriber, & E. Souberman (Eds.), *Mind and society: The development of higher psychological processes* (pp. 79–91). Cambridge, MA: Harvard University Press.

Watzke, J. L. (2007). Longitudinal research on beginning teacher development: Complexity as a challenge to concerns-based stage theory. *Teaching and Teacher Education, 23,*106–122.

Weeks, R. M. (1931). Teaching the whole child. *The Elementary English Review, 8,* 110–112.

Weissberg, R., & Cascarino, J. (2013). Academic learning + social-emotional learning = national priority. *The Phi Delta Kappan, 95*(2), 8–13.

Williams, P., Blankstein, A., Dienst, J., & Siemaszko, C. (2018). 10 Killed in Santa Fe, Texas, high school shooting; suspect in custody. *NBC News.* Retrieved from https://www.nbcnews.com/news/us-news/texas-high-school-lockdown-amid-reports-active-shooter-n875341

Wilson, E. O. (1984). *Biophilia.* Cambridge, MA: Harvard University Press.

Wong, H. K., & Wong, R. T., (2009). *The first days of school: How to be an effective teacher* (4th ed.). Mountain View, CA: Wong.

Yackle, K., Schwartz, K. K., Sorokin, J. M., Huguenard, J., Feldman, J. L., Luo, L., & Krasnow, M. (2017). Breathing control center neurons that promote arousal in mice. *Science, 355*(6332), 1411–1415. doi:10.1126/science.aai7984

Yusuff, K. (2018). Does personalized goal setting and study planning improve academic performance and perception of learning experience in a developing setting? *Journal of Taibah University Medical Sciences, 13,* 232–237.

Zins, J., Bloodworth, M., Weissberg, R., & Walberg, H. (2007). The scientific base linking social and emotional learning to school

References

success. *Journal of Educational and Psychological Consultation, 17,* 191–210.

Zinsser, W. (1990). *On writing well : An informal guide to writing non-fiction* (4th ed.). New York, NY: HarperCollins.

Sample Lesson Plans

Principle 1: "I" Work

Lesson Title: Acts of Integrity

SEL Competency: Self-awareness

Level: Most appropriate for grades 4–8, but could be applicable to all grades with appropriate, teacher-created scaffolding

Objectives:
- » Students will write a definition of the term *integrity* in their own words.
- » Students will experience an opportunity to act with integrity.
- » Upon completion of this experience, students will discuss what it feels like to act with integrity.
- » Students will complete a journal-writing activity discussing what they learned and how they will apply the idea of integrity to their lives.
- » Students will brainstorm ways to become more aware of acts of integrity in themselves and others.

Engage: Tell students that they will be learning about integrity. Read them the following proverb: "Whoever walks in integrity, walks securely; but whoever takes crooked paths will be found out" (Proverbs 10:9, NIV). Discuss the proverb and ask students how they define the term *integrity*.

Explore: Share the picture book *The Empty Pot* by Demi (1996). In this story of integrity, an emperor from China needed to choose a successor. He told children from across the kingdom that he would choose his successor based on how they grew a plant from a seed he had given them. One little boy named Ling received a seed, planted it, and watered it each day. It never grew. When he returned to the emperor a year later, he was embarrassed. His was the only pot that was empty and showed no life. The other children's pots had large plants growing. When the emperor saw that the other children had plants in their pots, he knew that they had lied about growing their plants from the original seeds. The seeds that he had given them were dead. They had tried to trick the emperor, but he knew the truth. Ling was the only child who didn't lie. He showed integrity and courage. Ling received the reward, and the emperor chose him to be his successor.

Create a challenging test based on the story. Distribute the test, mentioning that it is worth a test grade and is very important to students' overall grade in the class. Leave the room.

Explain: Return to the room and collect the tests. Explain to students that the real test was a test of integrity. Did they cheat? Did they remain honest even when no one was looking? Ask them to think about whether or not they passed the test. Allow a time for discussion. Ask students how it feels to act with integrity. What benefits do they receive from acting with integrity even when no one is looking?

Elaborate: As a class, have students brainstorm other times when they have observed people acting with integrity. Discuss the challenges that kids face to be honest and good. Brainstorm some coping mechanisms and ways to maintain integrity.

Evaluate: Allow students time to reflect on this experience in their journals. Give them a journal prompt or sentence frame if needed to support their writing process. Use a journal writing rubric to assess their work. End the class with a final discussion of the term *integrity*. Brainstorm ways for students to become more aware of acts of integrity in themselves and others. Agree on a community/classroom definition. Post the definition in your classroom for all to see. Consider posting ongoing acts of integrity underneath the term, increasing self-awareness in this area.

Principle 2: Creativity

Lesson Title: Design Thinking for Change

SEL Competencies: Social awareness, responsible decision making

Level: Most appropriate for grades 4–12 and adults, but could be utilized in grades K–3 with teacher scaffolding and family partners

Objectives:

» Students will use the design thinking process to creatively redesign a physical space in the classroom.

» Students will complete the design process by building a model of their new design.

» If possible, students will implement the design and create the new learning space using approved materials and methods.

Engage: Show some before-and-after pictures of classrooms or learning spaces. Discuss how the designers got from the before stage to the after stage.

Explore: As a class, walk around your classroom or campus and explore. Look for areas in need of improvement. Decide, as a classroom community, what space you would like to transform.

Explain: Using the following steps, teach the design process:

1. Start with the space as it is now. Define the problem. *Empathize* with the end user by considering the needs and desires of the learners who will use the space. Identify objectives and desired outcomes.
2. Next, *ideate*, brainstorming possible solutions to transforming the space.
3. Create a *prototype*: a drawing of the space and a design board with colors and textures to review. Allow some end users to give input.
4. Finally, *test* the design by creating a scale model. Allow some end users to give input.

Elaborate: Review the input that the class received, analyze the models, and make improvements. As a community, approve the final design for the space. Now, have students get to work and create the space, implementing the design. Encourage participation of many community members (e.g., parents, students, etc.).

Evaluate: Invite the end users to the space. Have a celebration and ask students to observe the reactions and the feedback they receive.

Principle 3: Cultivating Connections

Lesson Title: The Love Project

SEL Competencies: Building relationships, social awareness, self-awareness, self-regulation, responsible decision making

Level: All levels; K–12 and adults

Objectives:

» Students will complete 30 "acts of love" in an effort to change the culture on the campus or in their classroom. Each act of love will align with one or more essentials for cultivating connections.

Appendix

> » Students will participate in a panel, discussing the results of the project with one another and with an authentic audience of stakeholders from the school community.

Engage: Model an act of love in your classroom. This could be as simple as writing each child an encouraging note, sharing a story, or providing breakfast.

Explore: Ask students to discuss how it felt to be on the receiving end of an act of love. Make an anchor chart of all of the feelings and emotions that resulted. Discuss your experience of being on the giving end. Share your feelings and emotions, too, making sure to explicitly define any new terms (e.g., love, compassion, kindness, gentleness) that come from your discussion. Use child-friendly definitions (see Table 2 on p. 59) or let students create their own.

Explain: Explain "The Love Project." Tell students that, as a classroom community, they will attempt to transform the school by engaging in 30 acts of love over the next 30 days. Discuss the idea of love as the umbrella that connects us all. Discuss how acting in love helps build relationships. As a class, brainstorm a list of 30 acts of love to complete. As you build this list, link each activity to one or more SEL competencies. Here are a few ideas for acts of love:

1. Notice someone who needs academic help at school. Find time to help that person with his or her homework, sharing your own academic strengths with others. (Social awareness, self-awareness, and building relationships.)
2. Write a note of encouragement to someone who helped you. (Self-awareness and building relationships.)
3. Observe someone who is misbehaving. With love, redirect that person's behavior. Talk to him or her about why he or she might be acting that way. Think of a time when you were misbehaving and how you made a positive change in your behavior. Share your story. (Self-regulation, social awareness, responsible decision making, and building relationships.)

4. Create an "Acts of Love" bulletin board with ideas for your school community. Make sure to consider the real needs of the people in the school. (Social awareness.)
5. Make friends with someone who needs a friend. (Social awareness and building relationships.)

Elaborate: Direct students to complete the project. For the next 30 days, have them commit acts of love. Help students to chart their progress, noting the links to SEL competencies. Check in with your class daily.

Evaluate: Have students use personal journaling, a class diary, or a class calendar to record their experiences. Notice any growth in SEL over the 30-day time period. What transformations have occurred in your classroom and on your campus? Share your results on social media with the hashtag #teachservelove.

Principle 4: Writing

Lesson Title: Empathy Notes

SEL Competencies: Social awareness, building relationships

Level: All levels; K–12 and adults

Objectives:
  » Students will think about their friends and family members and select one person who needs encouragement.
  » Students will write or draw a note of encouragement, expressing empathy for someone's situation and offering compassionate words of encouragement.

Engage: Share with students a story of a time when you received an encouraging note. Share the note if possible.

Explore: As a class, discuss reasons why the person might have written this note. Discuss the writing/drawing process involved in the creation of this note, underlining the parts of the note and any critical academic vocabulary. Discuss the feelings that may have resulted from the giving and receiving of this note.

Explain: Teach the word *empathy*. Use a vocabulary strategy to teach the term (e.g., Frayer model, word wall, concept cube, etc.). Allow students to define the term using their own words. Use their kid-friendly definitions in your lesson when possible.

Elaborate: If age-appropriate, review the writing process. Discuss the writing timeline and allow students to move through the writing process at an appropriate pace with the appropriate supports. For English language learners and students with learning needs, provide a frame or template that will scaffold the writing process. For younger students and emergent writers, create the written text together, demonstrating the writing process, or allow students to draw their note using an illustration without text.

Evaluate: Allow students to create cards and write or draw the final draft of their note on the handmade cards. Then, have students deliver the notes. Debrief the experience, discussing feelings that resulted from giving the notes. Allow students to evaluate the importance of empathy in cultivating connections with others.

Principle 5: Breathing and Movement

Lesson Title: Compassion Conversation Walks

SEL Competencies: Building relationships, self-awareness

Level: Most appropriate for grades 4–12 and adults

Objectives:

- » Students will identify a cause to support.
- » Students will engage in a conversation about their cause, discussing reasons why they care.
- » Students will brainstorm a list of personal strengths that they might use to contribute to this cause.

» Students will begin to catalog their strengths and respond to a journal prompt related to the cause they selected.

Engage: Show a few commercials or promotional videos for some local causes. If you don't know of any, conduct an Internet search for volunteer opportunities in your area. This should lead you to find some organizations that are doing good in your community.

Explore: Give students an assignment to select a cause that they believe in. Give them an opportunity to create a visual representation (a poster or a video) of their cause. Allow them to share their visuals, justifying their choice. Why do they care about this cause or organization?

Explain: Explain to students that they will find someone in the class who is like-minded and shares hope for a common or similar cause. (You might have to help students find partners or small groups.) Explain to students that they will go on a "compassion walk" with their like-minded classmate. Define the term *compassion*, using a vocabulary teaching strategy to ensure and assess understanding. Give students a time and a route to walk, as well as guiding questions to discuss about their causes during their walk (e.g., "Why do you care about this cause?" and "What can you do to make a difference to this cause?").

Elaborate: After students complete the compassion walks, they should return to the classroom for a quiet, private time of journaling. In their journal, they should reflect on how they are feeling about the cause now. They should also write a plan for how they will move forward, considering ways that they can contribute to making a difference to this cause.

Evaluate: Debrief the activity. Discuss how caring about a cause might lead you to compassionate actions. Discuss the thought-language cycle, especially how talking about your feelings helps you decide what you can do.

Once the activity is complete, take a few moments and reflect on this lesson. Ask yourself the following questions: *Did talking with their partners increase students' compassion? Did talking increase their understanding of how they might be able to contribute to their cause? What is the benefit of finding like-minded individuals?* Follow-up with students to see if these conversations encouraged action.

Principle 6: Gratitude

Lesson Title: Acknowledgments

ESL Competencies: Self-awareness, social awareness

Level: Most appropriate for grades 4–12 and adults

Objectives:
  » Students will imagine that they are about to publish their first book.
  » Students will brainstorm a list of people whom they will thank on the acknowledgments page.
  » Students will write the acknowledgments page.

Engage: Find a few of your students' favorite books. Read aloud the acknowledgment pages of these books.

Explore: Discuss the pages. What do they have in common? Discuss the concept of gratitude. How would it feel to be thanked in someone's published book? As a class, brainstorm a list of people whom students might thank when they write their first book.

Explain: Explain the writing process that students will use to write their page. Use whatever writing process your students are familiar with or teach them one. Refer to the gratitude chapter in this book for ideas.

Elaborate: Using the writing process, allow students the opportunity to write their own acknowledgments page. Have students use a peer review process to help them develop their content and process their feelings of gratitude.

Evaluate: Share the pages in a public forum, either by publishing a collection of students' work or inviting an audience to a reading.

Consider inviting some of the people whom the students thanked to hear the students share their writing.

Principle 7: Holding Space

Lesson Title: Holding Space—A Practice

ESL Competencies: Self-awareness, social awareness

Levels: Middle school (with support), high school

Objectives:
- » Students will define the term *holding space.*
- » Students will brainstorm ways in which people have held space for them.
- » Students will experience space-holding during a class discussion about conversations on social media.
- » Students will write some guidelines for kind social media use and post these guidelines in the classroom as a visual reminder.

Engage: Begin a class discussion by sharing a kind message that you received on social media. If appropriate, compare that message to a cruel message. Discuss the importance of kindness versus cruelty on social media. Discuss the idea of social media as an environment where students can help others be their best selves. Use the term *holding space.* Students can use social media for kindness. When necessary, students can merely hold the space, creating a place for positive interactions and conversations (either by hosting a blog or by not tolerating anything less than kindness online).

Explore: Help students explore the idea of holding space in virtual and physical environments. Using a Socratic seminar method, pose questions that allow students to further explore their ideas about kindness on social media. Students should ask questions and refer to a text to support their ideas, such as "Teens, Kindness and Cruelty on Social Media Sites" (Lenhart et al., 2011). You can access this article at https://www.

Appendix

pewinternet.org/2011/11/09/teens-kindness-and-cruelty-on-social-network sites.

Explain: Explain to students that your job as the teacher during the seminar was to hold space for them as they had the conversation. You suspended judgment and created a safe environment for talking, feeling, and learning. Make clear how you accomplished this. Define the term *holding space*. Use a vocabulary strategy to help students understand what holding space means for them in your classroom.

Elaborate: Based on the conversation, have students write some personal guidelines for social media use. How will they choose to act in virtual settings? Let them write these guidelines for their own awareness about the importance of choosing kindness over cruelty.

Evaluate: Post the guidelines in your classroom. Periodically check in with students. Have them reflect in their journals about how they are applying the guidelines to their lives.

Principle 8: Commit-to-One

Lesson Title: My Life List—Dream Big, Start Small

SEL Competencies: Self-awareness, self-regulation, building relationships, responsible decision making

Level: Middle school and high school students

Objectives:
>   Students will read John Goddard's life list and engage in a class discussion of how he accomplished so much.
>   Students will write their own life list.
>   Students will choose one item on the list to accomplish and add it to the class calendar.
>   Students will celebrate one another's accomplishments.

Engage: Discuss the idea of "bucket lists." Share John Goddard's life list (https://www.johngoddard.info/life_list.htm). There are 127

events on this epic list. Have students note how many he accomplished. Discuss how he went about doing this. (He committed to one thing at a time.)

Explore: Goddard's list is broken down into categories. Explore each of the categories: explore, study, climb, photograph, explore underwater, visit, swim in, accomplish. Allow students time to research and begin to dream about what their own life lists would look like.

Explain: Explain the idea of commit-to-one. Show students some examples of how people meet commitments: goal journals, calendars, reminders on phones, etc. Discuss the importance of backward planning for achieving your dreams. Set a goal, determine what steps will get you there, and do the steps one at a time.

Elaborate: Students will create their own life lists of 127 things. Students will decide to start with one thing. They will plan the first step of the first thing and commit. Create a class calendar and have your students write their commitments on the calendar.

Evaluate: Check in with students. Periodically celebrate students' commitments.

About the Author

Season Mussey, Ed.D., loves teaching and learning. She believes that empowering teachers will improve schools, bring hope to families, and transform communities. She has a B.A. in Biology, an M.A. in curriculum design, and an Ed.D. in teaching and learning. She is an education consultant in Austin, TX, where she lives with her beloved family and dog, Darwin.